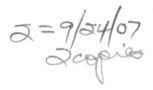

TEENS PARENTING
YOUR BABY'S
FIRST YEAR

Other Books by Jeanne Warren Lindsay:

*Teenage Couples—Caring, Commitment and Change:
How to Build a Relationship that Lasts*
*Teenage Couples—Coping with Reality: Dealing with
Money, In-Laws, Babies and Other Details of Daily Life*
Teens Parenting—The Challenge of Toddlers
Teen Dads: Rights, Responsibilities and Joys
Do I Have a Daddy? A Story About a Single-Parent Child
School-Age Parents: Challenge of Three-Generation Living
Parents, Pregnant Teens and the Adoption Option
Pregnant Too Soon: Adoption Is an Option
Open Adoption: A Caring Option

By Jeanne Lindsay and Jean Brunelli
Teens Parenting—Your Pregnancy and Newborn Journey
(Also available in Easier Reading [RL 3] edition.)
Translated by Argentina Palacios:
*Adolescentes como padres—La jornada de tu embarazo
y el nacimiento de tu bebé*

By Jeanne Lindsay and Sally McCullough:
Teens Parenting—Discipline from Birth to Three

By Jeanne Lindsay and Sharon Rodine:

*Teen Pregnancy Challenge, Book One:
Strategies for Change*
*Teen Pregnancy Challenge, Book Two:
Programs for Kids*

By Jeanne Lindsay and Catherine Monserrat:
*Adoption Awareness: A Guide for Teachers,
Counselors, Nurses and Caring Others*

TEENS PARENTING
YOUR BABY'S
FIRST YEAR

A How-to-Parent Book
Especially for Teenage Parents

Jeanne Warren Lindsay, MA, CHE

Morning
Glory
Press

Buena Park, California

Teens Parenting—Your Baby's First Year
is part of a series. Other titles are:
Teens Parenting—Your Pregnancy and Newborn Journey
(Available in regular, Easier Reading and Spanish editions)
Teens Parenting—The Challenge of Toddlers
Teens Parenting—Discipline from Birth to Three
Teen Dads: Rights, Responsibilities and Joys

Library of Congress Cataloging-in-Publication Data
Lindsay, Jeanne Warren.
    Teens parenting--your baby's first year : a how-to-parent book
especially for teenage parents / Jeanne Warren Lindsay.
    192 p.
    Includes bibliographical references and index.
    ISBN 0-930934-53-9 : $15.95. -- ISBN 0-930934-52-0 : $9.95
    1. Teenage parents--United States. 2. Child rearing--United
States. 3. Infants--United States. I. Title.
HQ759.64.L57 1991
649'.122--dc20

91-21513
CIP

MORNING GLORY PRESS, INC.
6595 San Haroldo Way   Buena Park, CA 90620-3748
(714) 828-1998
Printed and bound in the United States of America

Contents

ACKNOWLEDGMENTS

I am grateful to Mary Ann Shiner, Ann Ellwood, Nancy Bare-Knepshield, Sally McCullough, Jean Brunelli, and Sue Manzo who made time to read and critique this manuscript. Their comments were invaluable.

Perhaps even more important is the input from pregnant and parenting teens, the young people we interviewed, and whose wisdom is scattered throughout the book. Sixty-six young people are quoted, and many of them gave us permission to include their names.

They include Isabel Torres, Molina Lopez, David Munoz, Eddie Saldana, Chris Cardena, Alex Gutierrez, Holly Buchanan, Michelle Balderrama, Dora Alves, Selena Diaz, Lorena Martinez Silva, Lynetta Allen, Christi Gifford, Cynthia and Roman Mendoza, Pao Chen, Luby Ventura, Therese Albert, Albert Aguilar, Angela Cardena, Santiago Sandoval, Yvette Comacho, Virginia Palapil, Abbie Castillo, and David Lena.

We interviewed others who are quoted and acknowledged in the other books in the *Teens Parenting* series.

David Crawford, teacher in the Teen Mother Program, William Daylor High School, Sacramento, supplied almost all of the photographs. His models were his wonderful students.

Tim Rinker is the cover artist, and Steve Lindsay helped design the book. We appreciate so much the contributions of all of these talented people.

Carole Blum and Marlene Boehm again helped with the proof-reading and kept Morning Glory Press alive and well during book production time. Pati and Erin Lindsay helped with the proof-reading, too. We thank them for their valuable support.

I'm especially grateful to Bob who continues to be supportive even during those times when the current book seems all-important. I think he knows he's even *more* important to me.

Jeanne Lindsay

Preface

Nearly half a million teenagers deliver babies each year in the United States, and many of the fathers of these babies are also teenagers. Yet most parenting books are written as if all parents are adults.

A parent who is still an adolescent is part of two worlds, and these two worlds may be in conflict. A teenage parent's life is quite different from the lives of her/his non-parent peers. It may also be quite different from the young families who delay childbearing until both parents have completed their education and are able to form their own household.

I have worked with hundreds of pregnant and parenting teenagers during the past twenty years. Because our school district provides an infant center to care for their babies, many of these young mothers continue attending school on our campus after they deliver.

Many have fallen into parenthood accidentally, but it is
no accident that many are good parents. They've had help
along the way from their families and their community,
and, most important, they work hard at their parenting job.

This book is a parenting guide especially designed for
teenage parents. A major part of it are the comments and
parenting suggestions from young people who are "practicing" parents, teenagers who have children of their own.

Some are married, some are single. Whatever their
marital status, they are more likely to have money problems
than are older parents. Many live with their own parents
because of their age and/or lack of money.

Names of parents, their children, and a few personal
details have been changed in the quotes in order to protect
confidentiality. Parents' and children's ages have not been
changed. Their comments are real, and quotes are almost
always in the exact words used by the young parent.

Your Baby's First Year is part of a four-book series for
pregnant and parenting teens. Other titles are *Your Pregnancy and Newborn Journey* co-authored by Jean Brunelli,
PHN, *Discipline from Birth to Three* co-authored by Sally
McCullough, and *The Challenge of Toddlers*.

Chapter 5 of *Your Baby's First Year* is written directly
to teen fathers while Chapter 6 focuses on the special needs
of mothers who parent alone. The rest of the book applies
both to single parents and to couples who are parenting
together.

Parenting at 15, or even 17, is an extremely difficult
task. In fact, parenting at any age is quite a challenge for
most of us. I hope this book will help young parents
understand a little better the world of babies during that
all-important first year of parenting.

Jeanne Warren Lindsay   June, 1991

Foreword

Once upon a time, not too long ago, I lived, along with a number of other young parents, on a street we laughingly nicknamed Fertility Street. It was one of a seeming infinity of such streets in the United States.

Grown-up mothers and fathers and their large families of children lived in the houses on Fertility Street. Together. dads went off to work for pay each day. They thought of themselves as Wage Earners. Moms worked at home and were Home Makers. Children walked off to school, well-fed, rosy, and ready to learn. They came home for lunch. Every day. They were called Carefree Children.

Sound quaint? Yet it wasn't too long ago. I'm still alive, and I remember the way it was.

Today's children have a new descriptive label, "At Risk." The label doesn't refer just to FAS (Fetal Alcohol

Syndrome) or Crack babies whose brains may have been permanently damaged by prebirth drug addiction. Nor are we speaking only of children who have been abandoned or abused by crazed or uncaring parents. We're talking about babies who are born at risk because their parents, although they love their children deeply, simply haven't had the opportunity to learn the parenting skills necessary to give their little ones the basics for a successful life.

Teenage parents want to be good parents. Jeanne Lindsay's *Teens Parenting—Your Baby's First Year* can help them meet that goal.

Jeanne Lindsay has made a career of teaching teen parents, and the family life educators who also teach teen parents, how to give children the best possible start toward healthy and satisfying living. She possesses not only formal academic credentials, but also a practical loving kind of expertise learned as the mother of five children. She, too, lived on a not-so-long-ago Fertility Street. Her collaborators are teen parents who share their real life solutions to parenting problems. Readers have access to a kind of extended family in book format—one that is knowledgeable, and warmly caring.

In his book, *The Disappearance of Childhood,* Neil Postman has said, "Children are the living messages we send to a time we will not see." Jeanne Lindsay's easily read little volume helps ensure that at least some of those messages will arrive in good condition empowered to make valuable contributions.

Martha Bullock Lamberts, Ph.D., C.H.E.
Human Development Specialist
Rural Sociology; Child, Consumer and Family Studies;
and Cooperative Extension
Washington State University

To the young parents
who share so freely on these pages

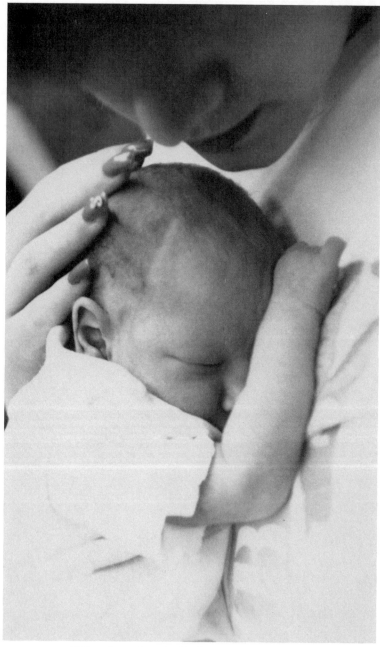

"When he makes the slightest cry, I wake up."

Beginning Life With Your Baby

That first month wasn't as hard as everybody told me it would be. I came home the day after he was born. The house was full of people during those first two weeks, and that was the worst part of it. I wish they could have waited until a couple of weeks after he was born. I was real tired. It doesn't seem like you ever really sleep like you used to.

You get home, and he's so tiny you breastfeed every two hours. I was worn out, but my mom cooked for me and kept things clean. I had no energy at all.

It's funny—nothing would ever wake me up before, but when he makes the slightest cry, I wake up. I don't sleep like I used to. I'll be in the kitchen, the washer is going, noise everywhere, and I'll hear him.

Adriana, 16 - Danny, 3 1/2 months

A Blur of Tiredness

Those first weeks with your new baby may seem like a
blur, a time of constant activity and tiredness. Your baby
may need to be fed every couple of hours. She may be
awake much of the night, then sleep most of the day.

*Have patience with her. The first couple of weeks I
was impatient because I wanted to sleep, and Jenny
wouldn't sleep.*

*Sleep while your baby is sleeping. I had to wash
clothes, hang them up, fold them, wash the dishes.
You don't have time to sleep, but you have to make
time. Sleep was important to me.*

Rosita, 18 - Jenny, 4 weeks

When you come home from the hospital, you will probably be tired, and baby's demands won't give you much
time to rest. If you had an episiotomy (small cut made to
enlarge the vaginal opening), your stitches may hurt the
first few days.

If you had a C-section, your recovery from childbirth
will be slower.

*It was hard when I first came home. I was in pain
at first, and sitting was hard. Nick wasn't that much
trouble, except the whole first month he had his days
and nights all mixed up.*

Theresa, 16 - Nick, 6 months

Most parents experience these feelings. Most parents
also experience the joy of early parenting. Holding your
tiny helpless baby is a special and usually wonderful
feeling.

Life with a newborn is described in more detail in *Teens
Parenting—Your Pregnancy and Newborn Journey* (1991:
Morning Glory Press).

Let Dad Help

If you're with your baby's father, whether or not you're married and/or living together, encourage him to be involved in baby care. When he is, everyone wins. You'll have some of the help you need with baby. The more dad does with baby, the faster he'll bond with his child. Your baby wins by having two loving parents.

Babies want all of your attention. Jay's father lives with us and does his fair share. He changes his diapers, gives him a bath, feeds him. He's a real good father—he loves him very much.

Bev, 17 - Jay, 8 months

Be careful that you, the baby's mom, don't suggest through words or actions that only you know what to do when baby cries. If you criticize your husband/boyfriend, he may soon decide that caring for baby is, indeed, your job, not his to share.

"He's a real good father—he loves him very much."

You'll end up getting tired and perhaps feeling upset. He may decide he's not needed, and that he's being left out of this whole parenting business.

Perhaps he hasn't had much experience with tiny infants. If he seems afraid of doing the wrong thing, show him how to diaper, feed, and rock baby. With practice, he may feel better about the whole situation.

We shared the night feedings. Luckily Dustin started sleeping through the night real soon. We did it all together.

I don't think it would be fair if I just said I'm not getting up, I'm not going to give him a bottle. We shared the responsibility of having him. I think you have to go 50-50.

Mark, 22 - Dustin, 21/2 (Kelly Ellen, 20)

Three-Generation Living

If you live with your parents, they may provide some help with childcare. If baby's father isn't around, you may need more help from grandma. Many young mothers who live with their parents find the first couple of months with a baby somewhat of a "honeymoon" period. Your parents may be eager to help you. If you have brothers and sisters, they may fight over who gets to hold the baby next.

After I had Elena I didn't go through baby blues a lot, but I didn't want people holding her. They'd pick her up and I'd say, "Okay, that's enough." I wanted her all to myself, and I'd get mad. I can't see myself doing that now. My sister would hold her for five minutes, and then I'd want her back. That was weird.

Monica, 18 - Elena, 23 months

Sometimes young mothers have more help than they want. If this happens to you, perhaps you can help your family understand that all of you—your parents, siblings, baby, and you—will be better off if you take the primary responsibility for caring for your child. If you start out, tired as you are, showing them that you know how to be a good parent, they may be less likely to give you more help and advice than you feel you need.

For more ideas on living with your parents and your baby, see *School-Age Parents: The Challenge of Three-Generation Living* (1990: Morning Glory Press). Teen parents and their parents talk about working out problems that may arise when a teenager brings her (or his) baby home to live. Both you and your parents might like to read the book.

Take Care of You Too!

If you have a baby to care for, you especially need to take good care of yourself. If you're breastfeeding, it may seem an all-consuming task. Your nipples may be tender at first. You may be self-conscious about feeding your baby in front of anyone else.

If for some reason you can't drink milk,
you can still breastfeed.

While you're breastfeeding, it's extra important that you eat the nutritious foods you needed while you were pregnant. You need about 500 extra calories each day. A sandwich and two extra glasses of milk in addition to your "regular" nutritious diet should be enough.

Drink enough liquids, too. You need 12 to 16 glasses daily of water, milk, fruit juices, etc. "Liquids" is the key word. You probably will drink a lot of milk while you're breastfeeding, but if for some reason you can't, you can still breastfeed. You need to get enough calcium some other way, but it doesn't necessarily take milk to make milk.

It's best for the baby if you can limit your drinking of
coffee, tea, and soft drinks to two cups each day.

If you're breastfeeding, it's better not to give your baby
a bottle during the first two or three weeks. Let your breasts
get adjusted to feeding first.

*I'm breastfeeding Jenny. Once in awhile I give her
a bottle. I figure God intended me to breastfeed, that
it's the right kind of milk for my baby. And I haven't
had any problems with breastfeeding.*

*It seems like I'm closer to her when I breastfeed
her because she looks at me and sometimes she
smiles. And in the night I don't have to warm any
bottle, just breastfeed her.*

Rosita

When you nurse your baby, sit (or lie) in a comfortable
place. Put your feet up and enjoy your baby. Drink one of
those many glasses of liquid you need each day. Learn to
relax while you're feeding baby. Your milk comes in more
easily if you're relaxed. Baby will be pleased!

It's absolutely necessary that you get enough rest if
you're taking care of a little baby. If you get too tired, you
may not be able to produce as much milk. Even if you're
bottle-feeding, your baby doesn't need an exhausted
mother. *Take care of yourself!*

Your doctor will want to see you four to six weeks after
your baby is born. Be *sure* to keep this appointment. S/he
will check your health and make sure you're recovering
well from pregnancy and delivery. If you haven't already
talked with your doctor about birth control, this is a good
time to do so.

Call WIC for Food Expense Help

If it's hard for you to get enough of the right foods for
yourself while you're breastfeeding, call your Public Health

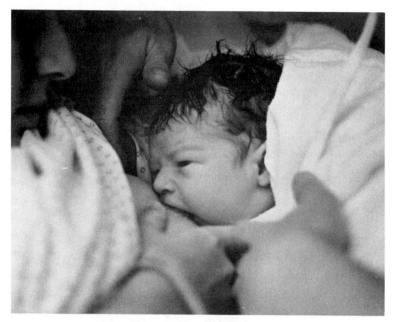

"I feel closer to her when I breastfeed."

Department for information about WIC (Special Supplemental Feeding Program for Women, Infants, and Children). You may be able to get coupons for certain foods you need. In many communities, the fact that you're a teenage mother may make you eligible for help from WIC.

WIC also provides help in buying nutritious foods for pregnant women and for baby's formula.

The Food Stamp Program helps extend food dollars for eligible families. Ask your social worker for information.

Peaceful Home Is Needed

In addition to simple comfort, baby prefers a generally peaceful home. If her parents argue a lot, she will sense it. She may become as upset as they are.

One young mother described her first month with her baby. She lived with the baby's father, and their relationship was not going well.

The baby cried a great deal which proved to be the breaking point in his parents' relationship. Kimberly was so tired from caring for little Karl that she had no time left for Tom. She also resented the fact that he refused to help her take care of their baby. Tom, in turn, felt left out and generally unhappy.

One night they had another terrible argument. Kimberly decided to take Karl and move back with her mother:

> *I stayed with Tom for two more days, but we weren't speaking. Karl was upset the whole time. In fact, he cried a lot from the day we came home from the hospital.*
>
> *As soon as we moved in with my mother, he started sleeping through the night. He's been an entirely different baby. Instead of crying all the time, he's smiling at us now. I know all that arguing was hard on him. I'm glad I finally found the courage to leave.*
>
> Kimberly, 17 - Karl, 2 months

Jeanne, mother of two-month-old Eric, explained:

> *Your home life has a lot to do with a child. If I'm tense, he is too. If a lot of yelling goes on, it bothers the baby.*
>
> *Sometimes Mike and I fight, but we don't in front of the baby. It's bad to do that because he can feel the tension, and it's not good for him. You would think a two-month-old baby wouldn't know, but they do. If they hear you fighting, it's bad.*

What About Family Planning?

> *Another baby? Not very soon. We want to wait three or four years. We're pretty careful with contraception because we don't want another baby right away. That would be hard because we'd be spending*

*twice as much on diapers and everything else. It
would make everything harder.*

*It'll also be easier when he's 3 or 4 years old
because he'll know more. He won't cry as much.
We've agreed to wait.*

Randy, 17 - Keegan, 2 months (Whitney, 15)

Couples need to think and talk about future family plans.
How soon do you want another child? Many young mothers, married as well as single, don't want another baby right
away. From a physical standpoint, their bodies need time to
recuperate from the last pregnancy.

Breastfeeding won't keep you from getting pregnant.
You conceive *before* a menstrual period. Even if you
haven't had a period since you delivered, you can get
pregnant.

See Chapter 16 for more comments from young parents
on this issue. Also see *Teens Parenting—Your Pregnancy
and Newborn Journey* for more information on family
planning methods.

Babies often come by accident. If you don't want to get
pregnant again soon, you and your partner need to discuss
your prevention plan. You either need to abstain totally
from sexual intercourse or you need to use contraception—
every time.

Enjoy Your Infant

The most important part of caring for your baby is
getting to know her—bonding together as closely as possible. If you interact a lot with baby—hold her, talk to her,
carry on conversations whenever she's awake, you'll find
the bonding happens just the way it should.

Your journey through parenthood has begun.

Feeding baby can be a time of special closeness.

More About Feeding Your Baby

Patty cries about the average. I don't always feed her because I can tell if she's hungry. I just pat her on her back and she goes back to sleep. She likes a pacifier, too. Sometimes she sleeps four or five hours. I'll feed her at 10 p.m., and she won't wake up until 3 or 4 a.m. During the day she goes three to four hours without eating.

I don't let her cry for long. My mom says I should so she can exercise her lungs, but I don't agree.

Beth, 18 - Patty, 3 weeks

Let Baby Set Mealtime

How often should you feed baby? Years ago, some "experts" recommended feeding her by the clock. She should eat every four hours, according to this theory.

Occasionally an extra small baby might need to be fed
every three hours.

We now think this was a terrible theory. Tiny babies
need to be fed when they're hungry. They can't tell time for
a few years yet, so their hunger pains are *not* clock-
directed. They're simply hungry when they're hungry. And
they *don't* cry to exercise their lungs!

*Paula only cries when she's hungry, cold or lonely.
Last night she was waking up every 15 minutes. She
wanted me to hold her until she went to sleep.*

*Breastfeeding is working fine. I didn't have much
soreness, only the second day when my milk came in.
I gave her a little water once, but she doesn't seem to
need that.*

Deanna, 15 - Paula, 3 weeks

During the first couple of months, most of your baby's
crying is probably due to hunger. Offer her your breast or a
bottle first. If she doesn't want food, naturally you don't try
to force her to eat. You look for other reasons for her
crying. But first you offer milk.

You'll find more about getting started with breastfeeding in *Teens Parenting—Your Pregnancy and
Newborn Journey.*

Breastfeeding for a Little While

Breastfeeding is generally the ideal food for baby. It's
also good for mom—no bottles to clean, no formula to mix,
and it's always the right temperature.

However, you may decide not to breastfeed at all. Or
you may choose to breastfeed for a few days because you
know how good colostrum is for your baby. Your breasts
produce colostrum for two or three days after delivery. It's
a yellowish substance which will help your baby fight off
colds and other illnesses.

Adriana breastfed Rachel for awhile, then decided to switch to bottles:

I stopped slowly. I'd breastfeed her when she woke up at 5 a.m. because that was more convenient—I didn't have to get up and make a bottle. At first, I'd give her a bottle at school, then breastfeed her at home. Then I had less milk, and it all worked out.

Adriana, 18 - Rachel, 3 months

Adriana was wise to stop breastfeeding gradually. Deciding to switch baby from breast to bottle suddenly is hard on baby and hard on mom. If you simply quit breastfeeding one day, your body will continue producing milk for awhile and your breasts will hurt. Baby will be unhappy at the sudden shift to the bottle.

It's far better to give her a bottle for one of her feedings each day for a few days, then cut out another breastfeeding, then another, until you're feeding her from the bottle all the time. You will both adjust to the change much better than if you switch suddenly.

Some Choose Bottle Feeding

Bottle feeding just seemed normal to me. I was smoking a lot, and they told me I shouldn't breastfeed because I'd give Mona the nicotine.

Ellie, 17 - Mona, 11 months

In a few situations formula is actually better for baby. If a mother must take medicine which would harm her baby, she shouldn't breastfeed.

If she is on drugs or if she smokes a lot, feeding her baby formula would be wiser than breastfeeding. (Staying away from drugs and cigarettes is, of course, the most caring approach.)

If you decide to bottle feed, you can choose from ready-to-feed, concentrated, or powdered formula. The ready-to-feed formula is the most expensive and the easiest to use. Whichever formula you choose, follow instructions carefully. Be sure bottles and nipples are absolutely clean.

Some babies are allergic to cow's milk. Ask your doctor if your baby seems to have problems. S/he will probably prescribe a formula made of soybean powder.

Heating baby's bottle in the microwave oven is a dangerous practice. While the bottle may feel cool, the formula inside could be hot enough to burn your baby.

Whether you breast or bottle feed, hold your baby close while you feed her. This is a wonderful getting-acquainted time for both of you. As you talk and smile with her, you'll feel even closer to each other.

Some babies need burping several times during a feeding while others don't want or need their meal interrupted. You'll be sensitive to *your* baby's needs. Several burping positions work:

- Hold her upright against your shoulder.

- Support her in a sitting position on your lap.

- Lay her on her stomach across your knees.

Whichever position you choose, rub or pat her back gently until she burps. For many babies, this happens fairly quickly, while others need several minutes of help with the important job of burping:

> *Keonia often has too much gas in her stomach. When that happens, I spend ten to twenty minutes burping her. If I don't, she'll spit up again.*
>   Lei, 16 - Keonia, 4 months

Offer your baby a bottle of water occasionally, especially in hot weather. Use bottled water or water you've boiled and cooled. Don't add sugar.

If he has a fever or diarrhea, he needs extra water. If baby has the hiccups, offer him a sip of water from a teaspoon. By the time he's four months old, you can try giving baby a little water from a small cup. He may be ready to take a couple of tiny sips.

Is She Getting Enough?

I pretty much fed him on demand every 31/2 to four hours. He was a good baby. He'd get up to eat at night, then go right back to sleep.

My cousin doesn't believe in feeding on demand. She says Orlando will get fat, that he'll be obsessed with food when he gets older. But Orlando knows when to eat.

Holly, 17 - Orlando, 5 months

How do you know if your baby is getting enough milk? If you bottle feed, your doctor will tell you about how much formula your baby needs.

At times, baby won't finish her bottle. You don't need to worry—she probably wasn't as hungry as usual. Her appetite will vary from feeding to feeding. "Enough" at one meal may not be enough next time. You will find she eats about the same *total* amount of formula each day.

If you're breastfeeding, your baby will "tell" you. She's undoubtedly getting plenty of milk if:

• She has at least six to eight wet diapers each day.

• She seems satisfied for at least one or two hours after each feeding.

• She seems to be gaining weight and is active when she's awake.

If your baby has been nursing every three or four hours, she may suddenly start demanding food more often. She's

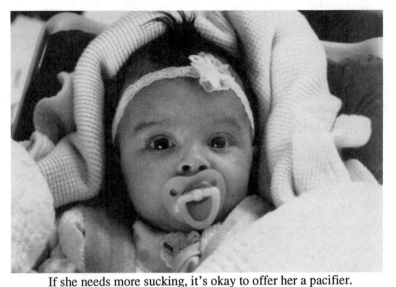

If she needs more sucking, it's okay to offer her a pacifier.

not telling you you've lost your milk. She's simply saying she wants more.

Nurse her more often—on demand—and soon your breasts will be producing more milk to keep up with her increasing needs. Then you'll be back to your three- or four-hour schedule . . . and your baby will again be getting enough milk.

No Propped Bottles—Ever

Whenever you give your baby a bottle, *always* be sure you hold him. Don't ever lay him down and prop his bottle in his mouth, then leave him to drink alone.

First of all, he needs the love and emotional support he'll feel from being in your arms. He also needs eye contact with you while he's eating. These happenings are all extremely important to baby.

I blew it with my mother-in-law yesterday. She's been wanting to keep little Eric for a few hours, and I finally took him over there. I thought he'd be all right while I did some shopping. I came back about two hours later, and I couldn't believe my eyes. My mother-in-law was working in the kitchen, and there Eric was on the couch—with a bottle propped in his mouth!

You should have seen him. His little hands were all clenched, and his whole body looked tense and uptight. Usually when he's eating, he waves his arms and has such a good time.

I was furious. I took a deep breath and said, "If you don't have time to hold him while he eats, I do," and I picked him up and went home!

Babies need to be held while they're eating. They need that love and attention. Besides, bottle-propping is dangerous—he could choke, and it could cause an ear infection. If she ever keeps him again, she'd better not prop his bottle!

Jeanne, 16 - Eric, 2 months

As Jeanne said, in addition to the loving he gets from being held while he eats, he's also less likely to have an ear infection if you don't ever prop his bottle. Many ear infections are caused by baby drinking from a propped bottle. The passageway from the ear to the throat doesn't drain well in infancy. Milk, if not "served" properly, can go back to his ears and cause an infection.

If you need another reason for holding baby while you feed him, remember that a baby with a propped bottle can spit up and choke on the milk curd. He's unable to spit it out if a bottle is propped in his mouth.

He May Need a Pacifier

Babies need a lot of sucking. Breastfed babies can probably suck more while eating than bottle-fed babies. If the milk in the bottle is gone, it's gone, while the breast

keeps producing a dribble of milk. A baby who needs lots
of sucking can get it there.

Lots of babies, however, whether breastfed or bottle-fed,
need still more sucking. Your baby may find her fist soon
after birth. (Many babies suck their thumbs while still in
mother's womb.)

If she seems to want more sucking, offer her a pacifier.
Even if the neighbors frown, giving your baby a pacifier is
fine. Throw it away as soon as she doesn't seem to need the
extra sucking, probably before the end of the first year.

Just don't substitute the pacifier for the attention, food,
or diaper changes she wants and needs when she's crying.

No Solid Food Yet

Babies under four to six months of age don't need and
shouldn't have anything to eat except milk.

Their digestive systems aren't ready yet for other foods.
It's best to wait until baby is at least four months old before
giving him solid food.

Feeding a two-month-old baby cereal in the evening is
not going to help him sleep all night. It may make him
cross and fussy the next day because of problems with
digestion caused by the cereal. If so, he may be so tired by
night that he'll sleep better. But don't give the cereal credit
for the sleep.

Vitamin/Mineral Supplements

If you're breastfeeding your baby, continue taking your
prenatal vitamins for two or three months after delivery. If
you do, your baby won't need an extra vitamin supplement.
She gets her vitamins through your milk, and an extra dose
wouldn't be good for her.

Vitamins. Commercially prepared formula contains
enough vitamin D for baby.

Fluoride. Whether you're breastfeeding or bottle feeding, your baby's doctor will probably prescribe a fluoride supplement beginning in the early months. Give exactly as prescribed. Don't overdose!

Getting enough fluoride helps prevent cavities in our teeth while too much fluoride can be a problem. It can lead to discolored teeth. Since the amount of fluoride in your water supply may be high or low, it's important that you ask your doctor how much, if any, fluoride supplement your baby needs.

Iron. If you're eating enough nutritious, iron-rich foods, your breast milk will provide enough iron for your baby for about four months. At that time, your doctor may suggest an iron supplement. Or s/he may tell you it's all right to start feeding baby an iron-fortified cereal.

Most commercial formulas contain iron. Your doctor will help you decide which one is best for your baby.

She's Changing Rapidly

As you care for your baby, you'll see tremendous changes during her first weeks "on the outside." You're working hard and you may be exhausted, but watching her develop makes it all worthwhile:

Racquelle is seven weeks old now. She looks more like a little girl, and she's a lot bigger than when she was born. At first I was holding her constantly. Now I lay a blanket down, and she's content to lie there.

Cheryl, 15 - Racquelle, 2 months

Be sure you talk to your baby from the minute she's born. As each week passes, she will respond more and more to your conversation. You, her parent, are the most important person in her world. Enjoy!

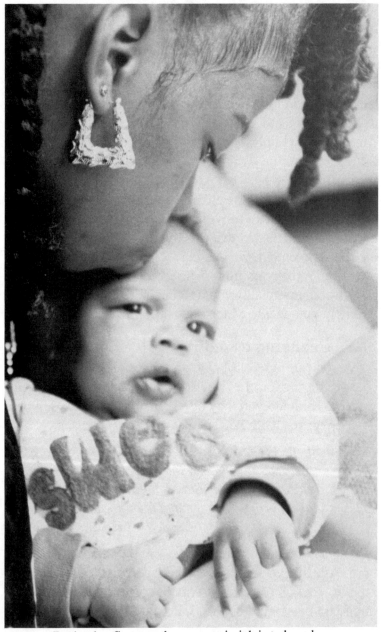

During her first months, your main job is to keep her
as comfortable as possible.

Keeping Her Comfortable

I think some babies get so bored. You see them and they look like they're spaced out. I think they need to be stimulated.

Play with them, talk with them, show them things, give them a lot of attention, and they will grow. I think they get real bored when they lie on their bed and look at the ceiling. Encourage them when they make noises by talking back to them. Find out what they like to do.

Ricky likes to be bounced on the bed. He likes his little legs moved, and he giggles. Then he gets so excited and he'll tell me about it. Or he will get into his moods where he coos for an hour, and the whole family sits around and admires him.

Courtney, 15 - Ricky, 3 months

Comfort Is Most Important

Your newborn's main interest is his own comfort. When he's hungry, he wants and needs to be fed—now. He may hate wet or messy diapers, or he may not seem to notice. If he doesn't like them, he lets you know by crying.

Even if you've fed and changed him, and you know he's neither too warm nor too cold, he may still cry. Often it's because he's lonely. Or he may be a colicky baby who just cries more than some babies do. (See page 41.)

Your main job as a parent of a newborn infant is to help him be as comfortable as possible. You feed him when he's hungry, change his diaper when necessary, hold him when he wants you to. But most of his days and nights the typical newborn spends sleeping.

I got a lot done those first few weeks because Dennis slept so much. People told me it wouldn't last, and now I know. He's 21/2 months old, and suddenly he's awake a lot.

We take him with us almost everywhere. Last week we took him camping for three days. Another friend with a baby went with us, and we took turns taking care of the babies. We had a good time.

Andrea, 17 - Dennis, 21/2 months

When he's awake and needs you, you're the one who talks, smiles, interacts with him. At first, he may not appear to pay much attention to you, but it's important that you talk to him from the day he's born. Your "conversations" with him help him learn to trust you and the rest of his world. When you talk with him, you're already helping him work toward developing his language skills.

Bathing Your Newborn

We know baby wants to be comfortable. To be comfortable, she needs to be kept clean.

Until your baby's navel cord drops off, she shouldn't be put in water. Just give her a "sponge" bath—lay her on a towel in a warm room and wash her with a soapy washcloth. Then rinse her off thoroughly and dry her.

Sometimes parents worry about that first "real" bath:

> *My mother gave Orlando his first bath. She offered for me to do it, but I let her the first two times. I was totally scared when I first bathed him. I would cry because he cried. I think he didn't like to be naked at first, but now he loves it.*
>
> Holly, 17 - Orlando, 5 months

Wash his head and face first. Don't use soap on his face, but wash his hair with plain soap at least once a week. After you've washed and dried his face, use your hand to lather the rest of his body with plain soap. Wash the baby's genitals just as you do the rest of his body. Rinse him thoroughly, wrap him in a towel, and pat him dry. Be sure you talk to him the entire time.

You might prefer to bathe your baby in the kitchen sink. It's a comfortable height, and you don't have to lift the tub to empty the water. Of course you have to be extra careful not to let baby slip and get hurt on the faucets.

If you live in a family home with a lot of different people, however, using the sink may interfere with their routine. If you do wash baby in the sink, clean it thoroughly before and after her bath.

Always test the water to be sure it isn't too hot. Stick your elbow in it. It's more sensitive to temperature than your hands are.

Never leave baby alone in her bath.

Even though some infants find bathtime relaxing and soothing, a lot of tiny babies don't like their bath. Sometimes when you put her in the water, she may shiver. If she

does, shorten her bath, then wrap her in a towel. And
there's nothing wrong with bathing a baby by using a
washcloth to wash her while she lies on the towel.

One mother referred to the first bath as "trying to hold
on to a wet seal." She continued:

> *A lot of girls are scared to hold the baby because
> he's too slippery. He's little, but he's a person too,
> and you shouldn't be afraid of holding him.*
>
> *Gary likes his bath now, and he laughs a little
> when I wash his hair with warm water. He cries when
> I take him out because he's cold.*

Leica, 18 - Gary, 31/2 months

Don't try to clean any body opening (nose, ears, navel)
with cotton-tipped sticks. Anything you can't clean with a
corner of a washcloth doesn't need cleaning. You don't
need to use cream, lotion, or powder on baby's body either.
In fact, some of these products may irritate her skin. Clean
babies smell good without the help of these items.

Don't worry when your baby touches his/her genitals.
S/he's curious about this part of his/her body. Touching the
genitals is as normal and certainly as harmless as touching
one's nose.

The Diaper Question

> *I was using _____ (big name brand), but now I'm
> going to the cheapest kind. I decided on disposable
> diapers out of laziness and because of the smell of
> having the diapers in the house. And I didn't want the
> mess of cleaning them out in the toilet.*

Bev, 17 - Jay, 8 months

Disposable diapers seem to be used "by everyone."
They're easy to use, and often are considered simply
another necessary expense of baby care.

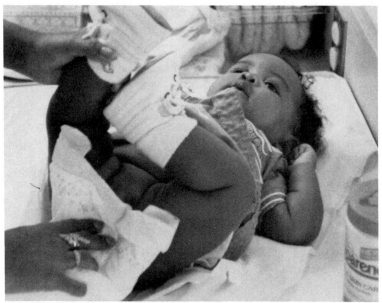

Keeping her clean and dry is important for her comfort.

It is still possible, however, and very respectable, to buy cloth diapers and wash them yourself. You'd spend less money. Cloth diapers are also kinder to our environment.

I use cloth diapers because of the money. Every week I had to buy a bag of diapers—nearly $100 a month! For 88 diapers it's over $20. I started using cloth when he was two or three months old.

I think a lot of girls use the disposables because they're lazy. They think changing cloth diapers is gross. Sometimes they're afraid they'll stick the baby with the pins. I use the cloth kind with the velcro.

Delia, 15 - Kelsey, 7 months

Before you decide whether to use a diaper service, disposables, or diapers you wash yourself, figure out the comparative cost in your area.

It is indeed easier to use either disposable diapers or diapers from a commercial service. If you have plenty of

money, take your pick. In any case, you'll probably want
one or two disposables and throw-away wipes in the diaper
bag for convenience.

Most of us would find several hundred extra dollars
quite welcome at the end of the year—and that's the difference in cost between using disposable diapers or the wash-
your-own kind. If you have good laundry facilities, washing diapers isn't hard. And you can always fold them while
you watch television.

> *I use cloth diapers. I don't like disposables. Robin*
> *gets rashes from paper and not from cloth diapers. If*
> *you rinse them out, they don't stink. I put them in the*
> *washer before school, and put them in the dryer when*
> *I get home. I fold them after she goes to sleep.*
>
> Melinda, 15 - Robin, 9 months

Dealing with Diaper Rash

During her first month of life, a baby should not wear
plastic pants for more than very short periods of time. Her
bed can be protected with waterproof pads. So can people's
laps—including your own.

The perfume in some brands of disposable diapers can
cause a diaper rash. If your baby has extra sensitive skin,
you may find the cheaper, non-perfumed brands work best.

When baby starts sleeping ten to twelve hours at night
(such luxury!), put two diapers on her. If she still wets an
enormous amount—her clothing and bedding are
drenched—you can triple-diaper, using a combination of
cloth and disposable diapers.

Change your baby often. Wash her with clean water
when you change her. The main cause of diaper rash is the
ammonia in the urine coming in contact with air. If she gets
a rash, it is even more important to wash her thoroughly
each time you change her.

You can put cornstarch or baby powder on her bottom after you take off her wet diaper, but it isn't necessary. If you use baby powder, don't shake it directly on baby. Instead, put a little in your hand first, then pat it on the baby. Baby powder shaken in the air can hurt baby's lungs.

There are both prescription and non-prescription remedies for diaper rash. You can get these either as powder or ointment. During the day the powder is better because, each time you change her, you can wash it off without irritating the rash. At night, however, when baby will sleep longer, use the ointment. It will give longer protection.

If baby has a bad diaper rash, let her go without a diaper as much as possible. If she's warm enough, let her nap without a diaper. The air on the rash will help clear it up. You can protect her bed with waterproof sheeting.

It's easier to prevent diaper rash than it is to get rid of it. For your baby's comfort—and your own—change her often. And clean her thoroughly each time you change her.

Babies and Colic

Some babies cry and cry, and it seems impossible to comfort them. Such a baby may have colic. If he does, he may seem to have a stomach ache and have attacks of crying nearly every evening.

His face may suddenly become red; he'll frown, draw up his legs, and scream loudly. When you pick him up and try to comfort him, he keeps screaming, perhaps for 15 to 20 minutes. Just as he is about to fall asleep, he may start screaming again. He may pass some gas.

No one knows what causes colic. It generally comes at about the same time every day. During the rest of the day, the colicky baby will probably be happy, alert, eat well, and gain weight.

If your baby seems to have colic, check with your doctor to see if anything else is wrong. If not, make sure baby isn't hungry, wet, cold, or lonely. During an attack of colic, holding him on his stomach across your knees may comfort him. Sometimes giving him a warm bath helps.

The good news about colic is that baby will grow out of it by the time he is about three months old. In the meantime, he will be harder to live with because of his colic. Comfort him as best you can, and look forward to the time his colic ends.

When Lance was a baby, he always had to be held. He was colicky, and we walked with him a lot. Then overnight at about four months he changed, and he was the best little baby. He was happy, and he didn't cry much any more. What a change.

Celia, 20 - Lance, 18 months; Laurel, 4 years

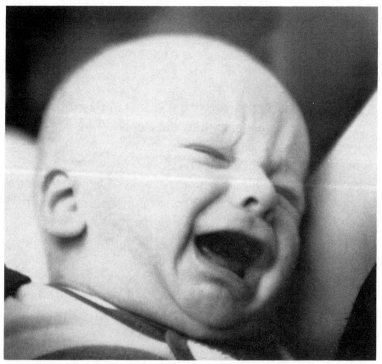

Babies cry for many reasons. Most often, he's simply hungry.

Why Do Babies Cry?

*The first few months I was having a heart attack
because it was all new to me. I'd say, "What's wrong
with him? I gave him his bottle. I changed him." Then
I would start crying. I would call my mom or my
mother-in-law. I'd get real nervous, but after the first
three months, we kind of got the hang of it.*

Ernesta, 20 - Jeremy, 3; Osvaldo, 5 months

Babies cry for many reasons other than colic. Most
often, she's simply hungry. The solution is also simple—
feed her. If she cries after being fed, is it possible she still
needs burping? Most babies can burp when you rub or pat
their backs gently for a minute or two. Others need to have
their backs patted or rubbed for a longer time.

Some babies cry because of a wet or messy diaper.
Again, the solution is simple—change her.

Other babies can't seem to fall asleep without fussing a
lot. If you're sure your baby isn't hungry, too cold or too
warm, and doesn't need her diaper changed, and she still
cries, she may need to be held for awhile. Don't worry
about spoiling her. Being there when she needs you helps
her learn to trust her world. If she trusts that her needs will
be met, she's likely to cry less in the future.

Important Note

Sometimes you'll do everything you can to help your
baby be comfortable, and she'll still cry. Always remember she is *not* crying to upset you. She isn't crying
because you've spoiled her. She's crying because it's the
only way she can tell you that she needs you.

Sometimes taking her outside will help. She may stop
crying if she has something new and different to watch. A
ride in the car (safely secured in her carseat) may calm her.

Some mothers report their babies fall asleep almost the
instant the car starts.

Some babies go to sleep most easily when they're in
their swing. Soft music might help. A little music box
beside their bed soothes some babies.

You May Get Frustrated

*Jesse was very fussy today. God, sometimes I wish I
could just get up and leave because I'm so tired of not
being able to do whatever I want. I'm trying not to
have these feelings, but I can't help it. I just wonder—
are they wrong? Am I a horrible mother for thinking
like that? I hope not.*

Frederica, 16 - Jesse, 5 months

Of course Frederica is not a bad mother for having these
very real feelings. Most of us get more tense as the baby
cries harder. The problem then is that the baby feels the
parent's tenseness and is even more upset.

Acting on one's frustration by hurting the baby is certainly wrong. Some parents resort to child abuse. For more
information on this subject, see chapter 10, *Teens
Parenting—Discipline from Birth to Three.*

When you're upset because of baby's crying, you'll help
your baby if you can possibly relax. Try thinking about
something you really like doing or fantasizing about your
favorite place. Your baby may relax as you do.

Sometimes your baby will cry because she doesn't feel
well. Is she feverish? Is she teething? See Chapter 7 for
more about caring for baby when she's not feeling well.

If your bottle-fed baby cries a lot, perhaps her formula
isn't right for her. Talk with your doctor. Perhaps s/he will
suggest a different formula.

As you get to know your baby, you'll find still other
ways to help her be more comfortable.

Other Caregivers

Some parents stay home most of the time with their newborn baby. Especially if she's breastfeeding, mother may find it easier as well as more pleasant for both herself and the baby if she doesn't try to take him out much or attempt to leave without him during those first weeks.

By two months, however, you'll want to go out, do things on your own occasionally. Unless you have a live-in sitter, you'll need to let your sitter know where baby's things are kept and the style of care baby needs. Does he expect rocking after feeding? Is he hard to burp? Does he whimper a few minutes before falling asleep?

In addition, be sure to leave phone numbers for your doctor, a caring neighbor, the fire department, and the police department. Put the numbers where the sitter can find them easily. *Always* let him/her know exactly how to reach you while you're gone. Some parents leave Medicaid stickers with a sitter if they're going to be gone long.

Whenever you leave your child with someone else, it's wise to give that person a signed medical emergency card. You could state, "_____ has my permission to obtain emergency medical care as needed for my child, _____." Generally medical care may not be given to a child without his/her parent's permission.

You Have a Wonderful Challenge

The first months with a new baby offer a real challenge to his parents. Your major task is simply to meet his needs as much as possible.

As we've stressed before, feed him when he's hungry. Change him when he's wet. Talk to him and hold him when he's lonely. He'll reward you by responding to you more and more as the days go by.

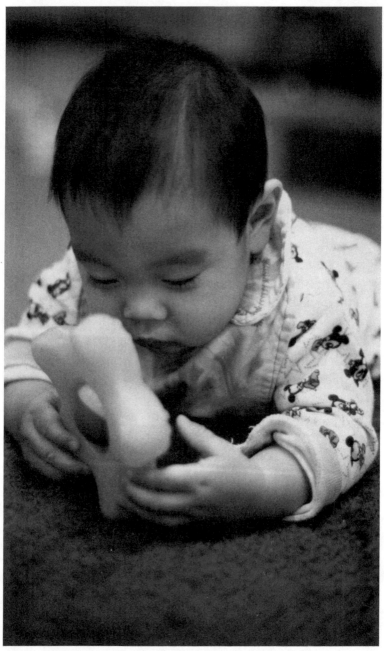

"Now he has a lot more personality—he's a real person."

CHAPTER 4

His World Changes

*J*uan *tries to talk back to you, and he makes noises. He's usually happy and has a big smile. He laughs out loud now, and he's so cute.*

He sleeps through the night. When he woke up in the morning, he used to cry right away. Now he plays awhile until I wake up. He sleeps with a bear, and when he wakes up, he talks to it. He goes all over the place on his bed turning back and forth.

Picking him up before, he was just there, but now he has a lot more personality. Now he's a real person. He's so strong you wouldn't believe it. He got hold of my ear this morning until it really hurt!

He loves his bath—even likes his hair washed. It makes him tired, too, makes him go to sleep.

Ginny, 17 - Juan, 4 months

By the time he's two months old, baby's world—and yours—is changing rapidly. By the time he's four months old, that usually sleepy infant turns into a little person who can "do something."

She's Smiling Now

Perhaps the most exciting thing a two-month-old does is to smile. If she feels good, she'll smile at almost anyone.

Four months is a popular age for taking pictures for baby food advertisements—and for sending to grandparents. You can almost depend on baby to smile and look great while you're clicking the camera. By this time, too, she will probably be giggling and laughing out loud.

> *About a week ago Gary discovered his feet. He pulls on them, tries to stick them in his mouth. He coos, yells, screams all the time.*
>
> *He's starting to laugh out loud now. He's happy all the time except when he's wet or hungry.*
>
> Leica, 18 - Gary, 3 1/2 months

You may stay home with your baby during the first month or six weeks. Soon, however, she will like going outside for a walk or to the park:

> *For the past couple of days we've been going to the Regional Park, all of us—father-in-law, mother-in-law, sisters-in-law, baby, husband, and I. It was so hot at home that we couldn't stand it.*
>
> *Barbi enjoyed it. She was in her stroller, and I took her for a long stroll around the park. She liked that. She looked at all the trees, and we had fun. We stopped at the playground so my sisters-in-law could play. I fed Barbi, and she went to sleep. We stayed at the park for nearly two hours.*
>
> Sandi, 16 - Barbi, 2 months

Hands Are Big Discovery

A big and important change occurs when she starts looking at her hands. Sometimes this is called "hand regard." At first, her hands are fisted, and she doesn't seem to be aware of them. She puts her fist in her mouth and sucks on it soon after birth, but this is more a reflex action, not a learned activity.

Soon, usually during her third month, she will truly notice her hands. She will hold one hand in front of her face and stare at it, sometimes for several minutes.

Stevie is beginning to look at his hands. Yesterday he looked down and got almost bug-eyed staring at his hand.

Alison, 17 - Stevie, 21/2 months

Carol sticks her hands in her mouth, looks at them, clasps them on her stomach. She started staring at her hands last Thursday.

Kristyn, 17 - Carol, 3 months

She looks at her hands now partly because she can see them more clearly. During her first month or two of life, she couldn't see small nearby objects very well. The world was a little hazy for her. By the time she's three or four months old, she probably sees about as well as any adult.

As her hands become less and less fisted, she will be able to move her fingers. This gives her something more to study. You may see her staring at her hands, moving her fingers back and forth, for five to ten minutes at a time.

Playtime

Paint a face on one of baby's little socks. Put it on her hand as if it were a puppet. Show her how she can move her hand around and make the face move.

Sometime during this period, baby will bring her hands together. Up until now, remember, she hasn't had much, if any, experience with those two hands feeling each other. Soon she will be able to pass objects from one hand to the other—a complicated behavior indeed.

A week or two after baby starts staring at her hands, she may begin to bat at objects. Hold a rattle five or six inches from her eyes. She will probably not only look at it, but she may also raise her fist and try to hit it.

She's changing fast. She's started grabbing things. She plays with her feet now, and she's a lot more active. She gets frustrated easily because she can't do what she wants. I hold her in my lap and try to let her see as much as she can, different pictures and things.

I read to her. She usually falls asleep. Now she wants to grab at the pictures. I have a couple of popout books and she likes those.

Adriana, 18 - Rachel, 3 months

This stage is the last time your baby will spend most of his time on his back or on his stomach. He will soon learn to turn over from back to stomach and from stomach to back. He's probably awake about half the time now, and he may seem happy much of the time. Illness, indigestion, and cutting teeth, of course, can cause unhappiness. Generally, however, things look good to a two- to five-month-old individual.

By three or four months, baby can sit up with support. Sitting upright gives her a much better view of her world. Think about it—how much could you see if you were usually lying down? What a difference it makes to be able to sit up!

Now Delphina likes to be propped up on the couch. I think it makes her feel big.

Tiffany, 18 - Delphina, 4 months

*Carol scoots. Sometimes I put her down on one
side of the blanket. When I go put clothes in the dryer,
she's off the blanket when I come back.*

*She rolls over both from back to stomach and the
other way. We help her with pillows. She can sit up
for a second, then she falls back down.*

Kristyn

If the weather is pleasant, baby will love going outdoors.
Lay her on a blanket under a tree where she can watch the
sunlight coming through and hear the rustling of the leaves.
Don't leave her outside alone, however, unless you're
working by a window very close to her.

Play with Baby

Babies like excitement—their version of excitement.
Instead of going to sleep right after eating, he now wants to
play. Now is the time to start playing regularly with baby.
If he's awake about half his day, he has time for a lot of

Play at this stage includes rocking and talking together.

interaction with you. Playing with him doesn't mean you get nothing else done all day. To baby, talking and singing to him while you work and he watches you is play.

The most important thing is your interaction with him. It doesn't mean complicated, time-consuming games—baby wouldn't like that yet. It does mean giving him your full attention part of the time.

Perhaps you'll gently tickle him, move his legs slowly up and down, or give him a variety of objects to hit and grab. He'll appreciate the attention.

Specific games with baby are fun, but at this stage, they need take only a few minutes. Patty-cake and peek-a-boo are the old standbys.

> *I play with Orlando—clap my hands, play patty-cake, sing to him, talk to him. He holds his head up now. He doesn't like to play by himself yet, so I lie on the floor with him. When he gets bored, I squeak the toys for him. He plays with his feet when he's in the infant seat. He loves to chew because he's teething. He's hanging on to things pretty well, and he chews on everything.*

Holly, 17 - Orlando, 5 months

Her first toys need to be big enough for her to hold easily, yet too big to put in her mouth. Her toys should be washable with no sharp edges or corners. Remove any parts that come off easily. Take out the button eyes on her stuffed animals. You can embroider charming eyes for the toys, eyes that she can't choke on or swallow.

If you've been around babies, you know how different each one is from the others. They develop at different rates in different ways. Some are very active, some are quiet.

Too often parents and other people think the quiet baby is the "good" baby. In fact, the quiet baby may need more from you than does the very active baby. She needs more stimulation to help her learn about her world because she's not likely to do as much active exploring on her own.

Help Her Exercise

We all need to exercise, even your baby. Give her plenty of opportunity to kick her feet and wave her arms freely. When she's three or four months old, she'll be able to hold her legs up. If the room is warm enough, she'll especially enjoy exercising without any clothes on.

When she's on her back, she'll soon start kicking. If she feels pressure against the soles of her feet, she may push against this pressure over and over.

You can provide pressure to her feet in two ways. First, if the end of the crib is solid, place her so she can push against it with her feet. Second, you can briefly stand her on a hard surface. She may enjoy pushing down with her feet for a minute or two.

She would enjoy your help as she exercises. Hold her feet gently and push her knees up to her stomach a few times. *Be gentle.*

Hold her hands—or let her grasp your finger. Pull her gently to a sitting position—if she's able to hold her head up. If her head is still wobbly, wait awhile for this one.

Help her roll from side to side on the bed. Gently massage her legs, arms, and body. She'll love it.

Playing Means Learning

Help your child do a lot of looking, feeling, and handling of objects. Perhaps more important, give him plenty of chances to socialize with you and other people.

Talk with him *a lot.* He will learn more easily later than will the child who spends these early months lying in a crib or sitting in an infant seat not doing much of anything. *So keep talking!*

Dad's relationship with his child can be very special.

For Dad Only

I was scared when she told me she was pregnant. I was working, but I didn't know how I was going to support her and the baby. I couldn't even support myself. I was also real excited. I was happy but I was scared.

I knew everything was going to be different. Nothing would ever be the same again. I felt like my freedom was going to be taken away. I couldn't come and go as I pleased, but I wanted to do the right thing. I wanted my daughter to have a father.

Carlos, 19 - Elena, 23 months (Monica, 18)

Many teen mothers parent their child alone. This book is written for them. It is *also* written for:

• Young couples who are parenting their child together.

- Young fathers who are involved with their child, or would like to be, whether or not they are still "with" their child's mother.

- Teen fathers who are parenting alone.

While most of these chapters are written to all teenage parents, this chapter is especially for fathers. Chapter 6 focuses on the special needs of mothers parenting alone.

If you're a teen father and you're reading this book, obviously you don't fit the stereotype of the teen father who gets his girlfriend pregnant, then takes no responsibility for his family. Whether you're married, living with your baby's mother, or not living with her, you probably are taking an important role in rearing your child.

If you and your baby's mother aren't married, it's important that you "establish paternity." This means that you both sign legal papers stating that you are the father of your child. If you don't, your child might not be able to claim Social Security, insurance benefits, veteran's and other types of benefits through you.

Your child needs your love and care. He also needs your financial support. Both parents are required by law to support their child.

Teenage fathers share their reactions to their partner's pregnancy in *Teens Parenting—Your Pregnancy and Newborn Journey*. The rights and responsibilities of young fathers, whether married to their baby's mother or not, are described.

Sharing Care of Your Newborn

Andy found caring for a newborn an entirely new experience:

The first time I had to change him was an experience I won't forget. I had never changed a baby

before. It was weird because I never had to watch
over anyone, something so small that was mine.
Before I hadn't even worried about myself, and now I
have to give him a lot of my attention.

Andy, 17 - Gus, 5 months (Yolanda, 15)

Fathers often get deeply involved in child care. Your
baby probably is a charming little person much of the time.
Caring for him can be rewarding for you and for him. In
fact, this can be a very special relationship for father
and baby.

Mario feeds Carol, changes her, and plays with
her. He even got up to feed her last night. He put her
in her crib, and she started crying. So he picked her
up and put her next to him, and she fell asleep. I'm
glad she's like that. I'm glad she's attached to
her dad.

Mario wanted to go fishing the other night. I said if
it was cold, the baby and I would stay home. He went
outside and decided it was warm enough, so we all
went to the lake. He caught a fish and showed it to
little Carol.

Let the baby get close to her father. It's really neat.

Kristyn, 17 - Carol, 3 months

The play between a father and his baby tends to be quite
active and generally includes a lot of talk. It can be especially exciting to the baby. Along with the activity, he
enjoys the lower pitch of his father's voice.

Even at a very early age, conversation between father
and baby will occur quite easily. The father says words and
baby responds with various sounds and facial expressions.

In some families, babies look to mother for nurturing
and comfort and look forward to excitement and fun with
dad. Both parents play a special role with their child.

Who Gets Up with Baby?

If dad is working and mom is home with the baby, they may agree on a traditional separation of work with mom taking care of the baby most of the time. Even then, having a tiny baby in the house, one who is awake and crying much of the night, makes it hard for dad to get enough sleep to be alert at his job the next day. (It's also hard on mom, of course.)

Night feedings? Diaper changings? I tried to help her, but I guess I really wasn't that great with me going to work. I was kind of a grouch getting up at 3 a.m. It was a lot of stress although Elena was a good baby. She got up more at night later.

The first month she would mostly sleep, but later when Elena got up she wouldn't want to go back to bed. It was hard for me to get back to sleep, too. I'd get up early and go to work, and I'd be exhausted. Gradually she started sleeping through the night.

On weekends I tried to spend as much time with Elena as I could, but I had to work a lot of overtime in order for us to manage. I can remember working 14 hours a day, and it wasn't a choice. I had to. I couldn't miss a day. Even when Elena was born at 5 a.m., after she was born, I went to work.

Carlos

Rene and Greg weren't living together when Vanessa was born. Greg was 19 and appeared pleased about the pregnancy. He worked part time the first year, and Rene continued to live with her mother. Because he didn't live with his child, he wasn't much involved in baby care.

When Vanessa was 9 months old, Rene moved in with Greg. Now they have a second baby, and Rene reports that Greg is much more involved:

During the week I get up with the baby because he has to leave early in the morning, but on the weekends he gets up at night. This was the deal we made before Shavone was born.

We weren't living together when Vanessa was born, and Greg kept complaining that he missed out on a lot with her. We talked it over when I was pregnant again—about the things he would do and what I would do. It's working pretty well.

Rene, 18 - Vanessa, 19 months; Shavone, 1 month

Making Time for Partner

Sometimes a new father feels left out because his partner seems to spend all of her time and attention on the baby.

I felt a little left out at first after Genny was born, but I never said anything about it. I felt guilty, too, when I felt like that. I got over it quick.

Miguel, 21 - Genevieve, 18 months (Maurine, 16)

He loves spending time with dad.

Mom can have some of those feelings too:

*He's very involved with her. In fact, he forgets all
about me. He walks through the door and goes
straight to her. I'll say, "Remember me?"*

*He plays with her, feeds her, changes her diaper,
everything. She looks like him. He's 23, and I'm 16.*

*He wasn't working when I got pregnant, but I think
the responsibility hit him. He got a job and we're fine.*

Marsha, 16 - Justin, 5 months

Many couples find it's hard to make time for each other
when they have a new baby. It's important for your baby's
sake as well as your own that you and your partner continue to work toward a stronger and stronger relationship.

If You Don't Live with Your Baby

You may have a close relationship with your baby's
mother even if you're not living together. Perhaps you took
prepared childbirth classes together. You may have been
deeply involved coaching the mother throughout labor and
delivery. Perhaps you're caring for the baby as much as
you can.

*I rock him to sleep. Now that he takes bottles, I can
feed him. I take him when Andrea gets frustrated. I'll
probably get more involved when he gets older. Right
now he's Mommy's baby.*

Ted, 18 - Dennis, 2 months (Andrea, 16)

If baby's parents are not married, how much "should"
father be included? If the young family lives together, they
probably feel much the same about joint parenting as do
married couples. If they don't live together, there is no
pattern cut and ready for them to follow.

Dad can still play an important role in his baby's life.
Shaun was away at college Monday through Thursday each

week during the first months after his baby's birth. He
spent weekends at his parents' home about three miles from
Bethann who lived with her parents. Troy didn't sleep a lot
during his first two months, and Bethann was exhausted.
Shaun decided he could help:

*I'm very involved with Troy. I take him overnight
once a week to give Bethann a break so she can catch
up on her sleep. This way, I get to be with Troy. My
mom or my sister help some, but I do most of it.*

*For some reason, he has trouble sleeping at
Bethann's house, but with me, he takes his bottle,
eats, plays, and goes to bed. He sleeps five or six
hours. I wish he'd do that for Bethann.*

Shaun, 19 - Troy, 2 months (Bethann, 17)

It's possible that Troy senses more stress at his mother's
house. It's also possible that having him only once a week
means Shaun has more energy to play with him. Babies
sense how a parent feels. If the parent is upset, baby
probably is too. If the parent relaxes, baby may do the
same thing.

> *Unless the court forbids it,*
> *you have a right to see your child*
> *and to spend time with her.*

If you aren't with your baby's mother, you can still have
a relationship with your child. Unless the court forbids it,
you have a right to see your child and to spend time with
her. If you aren't able to provide for her financially at this
point, share your time.

Work out an arrangement so that your baby's mother
also has some free time. Too often, the young mother is
saddled with the entire responsibility of caring for the baby

while the father doesn't even get to see his child. When this
happens, everyone loses.

How Do Mom's Parents Feel?

Mother and baby may live with mother's parents. Her
parents may have firm opinions about how much—if at
all—the young father should be involved. This can be a
difficult situation for everyone.

> *If Yolanda goes home and stays with her parents, I
> can't go over there and see my baby.*
> *When she's here, most of the time we take turns
> taking care of him. Yolanda isn't in school, so after
> school I go home and take care of him so she can
> sleep. Sometimes I take care of him on the weekends,
> sometimes she does. We take turns going out because
> most of the time if we stay at the house together, we
> end up fighting.*

Andy

Yolanda and Andy are under a lot of stress. Her parents
still don't like Andy, and Yolanda is not happy living at
Andy's house. They need to talk about their feelings, work
through this stage, and know that they may feel less
stressed when Gus is a little older. It takes a lot of effort,
determination, and love to make a relationship work at any
age, and especially when the partners are teenagers who
already have a baby.

What About Marriage?

What about marriage? Should you marry *because* you're
having a child together? Getting married because of the
pregnancy probably isn't a good idea. It's too easy for the
partners to blame each other when things get difficult later.
For this and other reasons, some couples choose to
delay marriage:

*We waited for marriage because I wanted to make
sure it was right. I didn't want to end up with a
divorce when he was 5 or so and put him through that
trauma. My dad skipped out on me, and I didn't want
to put my kid through what I went through. We didn't
want to rush into it. Her parents were real stressed
out, and they were trying to plan a wedding for us,
but no, no, we didn't want to go.*

Brian, 20 - Alex, 12 months (Erin, 16)

Brian and Erin were married when Alex was five months
old. Now Brian has a fairly good job and they have their
own little apartment, but it still isn't easy. Brian continued:

*I have a lot of responsibility now. I feel a lot of
stress. I'm 20 years old and I feel like I'm 40. We go
shopping and the baby gets this and Erin gets that,
and there may be $3 left for socks for me.*

Many couples find that the stress of caring for a baby
combined with money problems is hard on their relationship. Lei and Roy were married a month before Keonia was
born. Keonia has had medical problems including two brief
stays in the hospital. Lei takes most of the responsibility for
her care while Roy leaves early in the morning for work
and doesn't get back until after 6:00. Lei commented:

*I was never good with babies, but Keonia made me
understand babies' needs. Before she was born, my
husband and I were very close, but now we've drifted
apart and we seldom talk to each other anymore. We
argue more than usual.*

*Keonia makes me feel like I'm 30 years old. I feel
I'm not a little girl anymore or a carefree teenager.
A lot of times I feel that I'm giving all my love to my
daughter and there isn't any left for my husband.*

Lei, 16 - Keonia, 4 months

Hopefully Lei and Roy are able to talk about their relationship and make a conscious effort to regain their closeness. They may want to discuss their relationship with a counselor before they drift further apart.

Teenage Marriage: Coping with Reality by Lindsay is a book written for teenage couples. Reading it might give you and your partner ideas for improving your relationship.

Financial Problems May Occur

Financial problems tend to be intense for many teenage couples. Even if dad has a job, the money probably won't stretch as far as they'd like.

Brian, like many young fathers, works so hard supporting his family that he has little time to spend with his son:

> *When Alex was born I was only making $5 an hour, but I was determined this kid would be all right. I'd get two jobs if I had to.*
>
> *I didn't have a chance to discuss my feelings. I was on my own from the time I was 16. I left home. I didn't need anybody, and I was living pretty bad. I was living on the streets.*
>
> *I met Erin, and she kind of straightened me out. I got a job and tried to do something better with my life. I think it might have helped to talk with other young fathers, hear how they cope.*
>
> *I don't get to see much of Alex. I leave here at 5:30 a.m., and get home at 7:30, so I see him for less than an hour each evening. On the weekends we spend time together.*
>
> Brian

School Is Important

If you're still in school, you probably can't support your family by yourself. Most important for you right now is to graduate and acquire job skills so you can become independent as soon as possible. Many young parents continue to live with their parents until they're ready to be self-supporting.

Andy is struggling to finish school. Because there is no one else to care for their child, Yolanda is enrolled in Independent Study. Andy talked about their life:

I want Juan to grow good. I don't want him to be in the streets or nothing. I'm going to try to teach him what's right and what's wrong. I don't want him to grow up like I did or like my brothers.

We have our difficult times. She gets those weird ideas when we don't have enough money and we have to save for milk and diapers. Or when he's up crying at night, and I have to go to school. Most of the time when I'm up all night with him because he's sick, that's putting off my graduation.

When I go to school she mostly stays up with him during the day. Last week she got sick too, and I had to take care of both of them. Last week I was at school only one day because both of them were sick.

My mom and dad help me out a lot, but that's why I want to get out—so they won't have to worry about my baby.

Other guys—I'd tell them to wait until they're through with school and have a job. It's hard with no money. It's hard trying to go to school with the baby whether you're a mother or a father.

Andy

If you're already a father, you know that handling your responsibility is hard. Hopefully, you also know the joys that come along with those parenting responsibilities. Spend time with your child. You can be an extremely important part of his life.

"It makes it hard being the father and mother at the same time."

If Mom Is Alone

I would feel even more alone if the father had been with me throughout pregnancy, then left. But he left three months after I got pregnant. I'm not in touch with him at all. He's entirely out of the picture.

Sometimes I see a friend with her boyfriend and baby, and wish Orlando had a father. But other times I wonder if I'd want to share!

Holly, 17 - Orlando, 5 months

About two out of three teenage mothers are not married when they give birth. Some of these young mothers are quite alone. The baby's father may have left when he learned of the pregnancy. In some cases, he may not even know about the baby:

It makes it hard being the father and mother at the same time. It would help to have a father around, but there is nothing I can do about it. When Pedro grows up, I don't know what I'll tell him. His father never knew I was pregnant. I put "unknown" on the birth certificate.

My big brother is around, and he holds him. I think that will help.

                                          Maria, 17 - Pedro, 2 months

Maria had a tough time for three years. She continued living at home, and managed to go to school fairly regularly. When Pedro was three, Maria married Ralph (not Pedro's father). They now have four children including Pedro. The fact that your child's father is not around doesn't mean your child will never have a father. A "real" father is a dad who is actively parenting. Ralph is Pedro's real father because he is the one who has taken that role.

On Being Positive—and Honest

Do I Have a Daddy? (1991: Morning Glory Press) is a picture book for the child who doesn't know his biological father. Included in the book is a section of suggestions for a single mother. Young mothers share their thoughts on this important topic. These young mothers stress two things:

• Be honest with your child.

• Be as positive as possible.

For some young mothers, these goals are in conflict. Perhaps at this point you find it hard to say anything good about your child's father. Raylene is in this position:

I thought maybe because he is her dad, I should give marriage a thought. But I knew I would be getting into the same abuse my mom is in except Rick didn't drink. He was mean when he was sober, while my dad does it when he's drunk. I didn't even consider marrying him.

> *The last time Rick hit me was six weeks before*
> *Victor was born. I realized I deserved better. I would*
> *rather be alone and single forever than put up*
> *with that.*
> *Victor's father would say, "You'll never find*
> *anybody else. Guys will think you're a whore."*
> > Raylene, 18 - Victor, 2

Talking in a positive way with Victor about his father will be hard for Raylene. However, in *Do I Have a Daddy?* Robin says:

> *Why make a kid feel like his father was a louse? If*
> *his dad's a louse, that makes him half-louse. It's not*
> *fair to lay your feelings on your child.*
> *I tell Stu, "Your father wasn't as lucky as I am—he*
> *didn't get to live with you.*
> > Robin, 21 - Stu, 5

Robin is right. It's important for your child's sake that you try to look beyond your own feelings. This will be difficult for Raylene. She may decide to level with Victor at some time and tell him that she and his father had a very poor relationship. With the passage of time, perhaps she will also be able to share some positive memories with her son.

Filing for Child Support

Some young mothers choose not to name the father of their baby. They don't file for child support. "I can do it on my own," they say.

This isn't fair to the child. Even if the father has no job and no money now and you don't think you want your child to know him, it's still important that he not be shut out of his child's life forever.

Both parents are required by law to support their child, whether or not they planned to have a child together. A child supported by only one parent is likely to be poor. He has a right to benefits from both parents, benefits such as Social Security, insurance benefits, inheritance rights, veteran's and other benefits. You need to establish paternity so that your child will be able to claim such benefits.

In some states, paternity is established by both mother and father signing a legal paper saying he is the father. If the father refuses to admit paternity, you may need to go to court.

Blood tests are almost 100 percent accurate in identifying the father of a child. The blood tests are genetic tests which compare many different factors in your blood with similar parts of the man's and the child's blood.

Some couples are close throughout much of the pregnancy, then split up before the baby is born. Kellie's situation is typical:

We aren't together now but he's paying child support. He hasn't seen Kevin since he was a month old.

We had been together for two years, and we were close up to my eighth month. He was excited about the whole thing. Then his parents separated and his brother was getting divorced. He got scared that would happen to us.

He was back with me for about a month after Kevin was born, then left again. Now he's trying to come back. I'm not going to let that happen because I don't want Kevin hurt again, and I don't want to be hurt.

We had talked of marriage. Then in just one week we went from planning marriage to he never wanted to see me again. I think he's scared of growing up and taking responsibility.

*I wouldn't think it was possible, but his feelings
seemed to change overnight. I think it had a lot to do
with his mother. Once I got pregnant, she went totally
against me. I was fine, good enough for him until I
got pregnant. Then she decided I was trying to trap
him. We had a good relationship those two years. We
hardly ever fought.*

Kellie, 16 - Kevin, 3 months (Ron, 18)

It's impossible to say what Kellie "should" do. It's
possible that she and Ron will eventually decide to parent
together—or they may not. In either case, Kellie is wise to
have filed for child support. She also may decide, even if
she and Ron are not together, that Ron and Kevin need to
have a relationship.

Other People's Comments

Being alone during pregnancy and afterward is extremely difficult for many moms. Other people may make
it even harder:

*When you see someone with the father you just
want to cry because you aren't going to have a father
for your baby. I'd hear all of these girls talking about
the baby's father, and how we aren't together.*
*They would ask me questions like "Are you with
the baby's father? Are you going to get married?"
You have to answer them, and it's embarrassing.
Sometimes you want to cry right then, and they would
know they brought up a sad subject and would try to
talk about something else.*

Goldie, 17 - Jimmy, 3 months

You don't "have to answer them." It's okay to say, "I'd
rather not talk about it." You don't owe people an explana-
tion. On the other hand, sometimes it helps to talk about

our problems with someone we trust. When you're
parenting alone, having the support of a few close friends
can help a lot.

Having friends is also important if you are with your
baby's father. Maurine stayed with Miguel for more than a
year after Genny was born. She and Miguel were close, so
close that Maurine says she gave up her own identity for
awhile. She feels now that this was a mistake:

> *Girls need to learn not to be so dependent. I be-*
> *came terribly dependent on Miguel. Then we'd break*
> *up and I'd think I couldn't do anything for myself.*
> *You have to be responsible for yourself. It's hard to*
> *explain. You think he's everything.*
>
> *Until they have experienced it, a lot of girls aren't*
> *going to believe it could happen to them. That's what*
> *I thought. He was so good to me.*

A single parent can certainly be a loving, "good" parent.

> *You need to have contact with your friends. I
> didn't. I stopped going out with them and stayed with
> Miguel because he got so jealous. It's better if you go
> out with your friends and he goes out with his. We
> were together too much.*
>
> *I tell him I don't want to get back with him, but he
> doesn't want to hear that. That day when we broke up
> I felt different. I felt totally free. I like the way I feel.*
>
> Maurine, 16 - Genevieve, 18 months

Dependency is not a good foundation for a relationship.
Maurine and Miguel may get back together, or they may
not. In either case, Maurine's new-found freedom to be
herself is likely to help her build a better relationship in the
future, whether that relationship is with Miguel or with
someone else.

"I Still Like Him"

Beth has very mixed feelings about her child's father:

> *At first Al saw the baby about every other day, or
> called up to see how she was. Then I decided I didn't
> want him to see Patty any more. I told him, and we
> argued about it. He has the right, I know, and he
> really does care about her. I had thought he was the
> type of guy who would say, "So I have a baby, so
> what?" but he's not.*
>
> *Al had planned to coach me during labor, then we
> started arguing. The subject wasn't brought up again.
> I found another coach, a friend of mine.*
>
> *I haven't seen Al much for quite awhile. When I
> was first pregnant, we were going to get married. But
> I didn't want to get married just because of the
> pregnancy—I think that's a big mistake. Maybe when
> he works out what he wants to do with his life . . .*
>
> *Perhaps the real reason I don't want him to see
> Patty is because I still like him. When he's around*

*here I get really upset. So maybe if/when I don't have
these feelings, it will be the right time for him to come
around.*

*Now I still care for him a lot, and when I see him
with his daughter, I feel sad. I wish things could have
worked out. I know he has the right to see her, but I'm
not ready for it, that's all.*

Beth, 18 - Patty, 3 weeks

If the baby's father is providing some financial support
—and sometimes even if he's not—he has a right to see his
baby. Legally, he may be able to have his child with him
part of the time. If the young parents disagree on this
matter, they should talk to a lawyer or legal aid group.

Dad May Be Far Away

Sometimes the baby's father can't be with his family. He
may be in the armed forces, or he may be away for other
reasons:

*The father isn't involved at all. He's been in jail
since I was 6 months along. We write sometimes. Dan
saw the baby once when he was six weeks old. He'll
be out in January, and I want him to know the responsibilities because if he ever wants another kid, I don't
want any. We were both scared when I told him I was
pregnant.*

Elisa Marie,15 - Delila, 10 months

What is Elisa Marie's responsibility to Delila and to
Delila's father? Should she try to maintain a relationship
with him? That's a hard question, one that only Elisa Marie
and Dan can answer. If Dan is to have a relationship with
Delila, Elisa Marie can help by sending lots of photos to
him and keeping him up to date on his daughter's
development.

Handling Future Relationships

Young mothers who are alone may wonder how to handle future relationships. How soon should you tell a new friend about your child? Most moms agree that it's important to be honest. "If he doesn't want to have anything to do with me because I have a baby, he's not for me," they say.

On the other hand, sometimes a new boyfriend seems too eager to be a father to the child:

> *Dating other people is hard. I dated one person who liked me, but he thought the only reason I wanted to go out with him was for him to be a father to Kevin. Another one was already putting money away for his college.*
>
> *Finding the right person is going to be hard. It's going to have its ups and downs. I want to find somebody who's not afraid, but who doesn't want to take over the whole situation.*
>
> Kellie

Finding the "right" approach to future relationships can be difficult. You might like your child to have an acting father. At the same time you don't want her to assume that every man who comes around is going to be her dad.

When you have a child, handling dating and your relationship with a possible future partner takes a great deal of wisdom, love, and caring.

Single Parenting Can Work

About half the children in the United States today will spend at least part of their lives in a one-parent household. Most people still think it's better for a child to have two parents who care about each other. But a single parent can certainly be a loving, "good" parent. It just takes a little more effort.

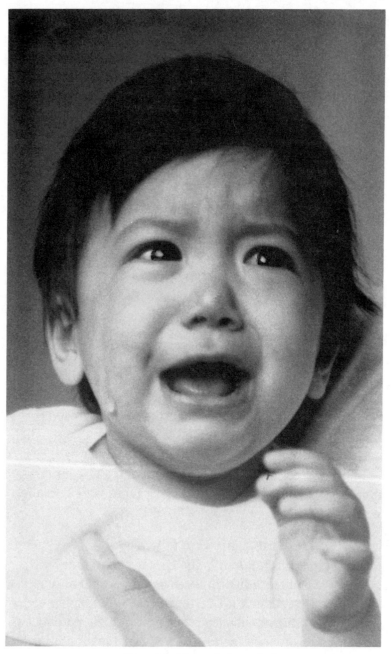

"I'm sick. Please help me."

Health Care
For Your Baby

Sometimes babies are sick. They have colds, fevers, and other illnesses.

There are also other serious childhood diseases, diseases that your child need never have. It's up to you because you can immunize him against such diseases as polio, mumps, whooping cough, and measles.

Importance of Immunizations

In the early part of this century two of the leading causes of death for children under two were diphtheria and whooping cough (pertussin). You don't need to worry about these diseases because of the DTP shots your child should start getting at age two months.

Oral polio vaccine is given at the same time as the DTP immunization. Red liquid drops are put in baby's mouth.

DTP: A series of immunizations
against three diseases:
- **Diphtheria**
- **Tetanus**
- **Pertussin**

He will have a series of three of these shots, usually two months apart. Tetanus is a disease related to accidental injury. He should get occasional booster shots against tetanus throughout his life.

Your baby will need additional DTP and polio immunizations when he's eighteen months old, and again before he starts kindergarten.

Polio vaccine has been available in this country for about 35 years. Before that time, thousands of children and adults became ill with polio every summer. Many of these victims died, others became paralyzed, handicapped for life.

The polio vaccine available to your child during the first six months of life can prevent this horrible disease. Polio is still prevalent in many parts of the world including Mexico, so it's important to have your baby immunized against it.

In addition, when he's 15 months old, your baby will need to be immunized against :
- "Red" measles
- Rubella (German measles)
- Mumps

Pneumonia and meningitis are common complications of measles. Some children have become permanently deaf from mumps.

Rubella (German measles) generally doesn't make babies too sick. A pregnant woman exposed to rubella during the first three months of her pregnancy, however, is at high risk of having a baby who is deaf, has heart disease, or some other birth defect because of the rubella. If the woman has had rubella herself or was vaccinated before she was pregnant, her baby is not in danger.

If your baby got rubella, he might give it to a pregnant woman, so be sure he is immunized.

Immunizations are free at the Health Department. They may be given by the Health Department at local parks. If you don't know where to take your baby for his shots, ask your school nurse for a recommendation.

Possible Reaction to Shots

Most babies have some reaction to immunizations. Usually the reaction lasts only a day or two and is generally mild. Giving your child a baby non-aspirin pain reliever such as Tylenol or Pediacare will help relieve these symptoms.

When Nick got his shots, he got a lot of fever—that really bothered him. He woke up at midnight with a fever, and I gave him Tylenol. That helped.

Theresa, 16 - Nick, 6 months

See page 82 for suggestions about caring for a feverish child.

Of course, if your baby has a severe reaction to his immunizations (high fever for more than twelve hours or other severe symptoms), you should call your doctor.

Be sure to keep a record of your baby's immunizations. You will need these records to enroll your child in school.

When Should You Call Your Doctor?

You call the doctor when you don't know what to do because there's something wrong with the baby. He might get upset if you overdo it—mine did once— but better safe than sorry.

Sometimes, if I'm worried but don't think there's much wrong, I go to another mother before I call the doctor. If she has a fever or seems sick, I call.

Melinda, 15 - Robin, 9 months

When should you call your baby's doctor? If you take baby's temperature under his arm (less disturbing to the baby than is sticking a thermometer into his rectum), and it reads more than 101 degrees, call the doctor.

The best way to take underarm (called *axillary*) temperature is with a disposable or digital thermometer. These are available in drugstores. If possible, use them to take baby's temperature. Otherwise, use a glass thermometer.

If your baby gets a sudden unexplained rash, call your doctor.

Many babies spit up occasionally during the first two months. This is generally a combination of lumps of partially digested milk combined with watery-looking fluid. They do this because their digestive tract is not completely mature. This happens more often with premature babies. He

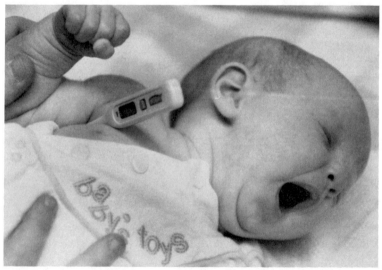

Taking underarm temperature with a digital thermometer works well.

will spit up less if you give him frequent small feedings and handle him extra gently after feeding.

Generally, this occasional spitting up is nothing to worry about. But if baby, after every feeding, suddenly vomits most of his meal, call your doctor immediately.

Diarrhea Can Be Serious

Diarrhea, which can be a serious problem for a baby, is not diagnosed by the number of bowel movements the baby has each day. More important is the consistency of the BM.

Diarrhea: a thin, watery, foul-smelling discharge

If baby has this condition for as long as twelve hours, call the doctor. A baby with diarrhea can quickly lose a dangerous amount of fluid.

Diarrhea is best treated by giving the baby clear liquids and nothing else for 24 hours. Liquids you should give him include Pedialyte (non-prescription liquid you buy in the drugstore or grocery store), clear water, or water mixed with apple juice (1 tablespoon apple juice to 8 ounces of water). Offer no solid foods, and feed him liquids as often as he'll take them.

Hernia? Check with Doctor

If you think your baby might have a hernia, check with your doctor.

Hernia: a bulge around the navel or the seamline between the leg and the tummy

You're most likely to notice it after baby has cried a lot or strained to have a bowel movement. Sometimes it will go away by itself, but occasionally it requires simple

surgery. If your doctor recommends surgery, it's usually
done during the second year of baby's life.

Her First Doctor's Appointment

Doctors generally have you bring the baby in when she's
about two weeks old. At this visit it's good to talk about
any troubles at all with feeding. If you have any concerns
with the baby's navel (belly button), if you suspect hernia,
or if you have other worries, tell him/her.

It's a good idea on your first visit to the doctor to learn
the names of the various people working there. If you know
the names of the receptionist and the nurse, you can call
them by name when you telephone. If you do so, you're
more likely to get a friendly response.

Above all, don't be afraid to ask questions. Write down
everything you want to discuss with your doctor. Is s/he
always in a hurry? Stop her/him and say, "Wait. I have
these questions, and I need your help."

If you briefly describe whatever is worrying you, s/he'll
take time to advise you. If not, perhaps you need to look for
another doctor who will answer your questions.

Dealing with Fever

Fever is one of the early signs of illness in a baby, and
you shouldn't ignore it. What can you do about fever at
home? Give the baby Tylenol or other non-aspirin pain
reliever as recommended by your doctor.

Cooling baths are another way to bring fever down. If
baby shivers while you're bathing him, it's too cold. A
good way to do this is to put a towel in lukewarm water.
Then wrap the baby in the wet towel. It helps bring his
temperature down, and he's less likely to shiver.

Lukewarm water is the best thing to use. Don't use
alcohol. The fumes can be dangerous for baby to breathe.

It's also important to give your child liquids when he has a fever. If it's a sore throat that's causing his fever, your baby may not want to do a lot of sucking.

> *That one throat infection Lynn had was terrible. I took her to the doctor, and they gave me Penicillin to give her. About a week later I took her back to school.*
>
> *She was really sick—she couldn't keep anything down. She couldn't suck the bottle because her throat was so sore. She cried a lot. We'd go to sleep, and she'd wake up 15 minutes later. Her crying got on my nerves, but when I picked her up, she'd quit crying.*
>
> Sheryl Ann, 17 - Lynn, 7 months

A way to encourage your child to take lots of liquids is to give him popsicles. If a little piece breaks off in his mouth, it will melt quickly and he can swallow it. This much sugar won't hurt him.

Popsicles are also good for babies and toddlers if they have a lot of nausea and vomiting. Sucking on a popsicle will often help. Orange and other fruit juices, of course, can be frozen to make your own popsicles if you don't want to buy the sugary ones. Besides being cold and making him feel better, homemade juicesicles are nutritious.

Ear Infection? Call Doctor

> *Jonita had an ear infection which made her congestion problem even worse. Yes, I used to prop bottles. My mom probably still props them.*
>
> Ellen, 17 - Jonita, 6 1/2 months

When your child has an ear infection, call the doctor. While a non-aspirin pain reliever can take away some of the pain and the fever, it doesn't kill the germs causing the infection in the ear. Only prescription medication can do that, so you need to take baby to the doctor. Most doctors, when you say "Ear infection," say "Bring him in." There's a real danger of permanent hearing loss if an ear infection is not treated promptly.

As discussed in Chapter 2, many infants' ear infections are caused by propped bottles.

Before you call your doctor, make some notes about your baby's condition. Then you'll be able to describe his symptoms more accurately:

- Is he coughing? For how long?

- Has he lost his appetite?

- Does he have diarrhea?

- What is his temperature?

- Has he been exposed to any diseases?

- Has he received all of the immunizations he should have had by this time?

If your doctor prescribes medication for your baby, be sure to ask if you should give baby all the medicine that is in the bottle, or if you give it only for a certain number of days. Most antibiotics (Penicillin, Ampicillin, Ilison) need to be used until they are all gone. However, decongestants such as Actifed and Dimetapp are to be used only when symptoms of congestion are present—when he has a stuffy, runny nose.

Colds Are Common

Most children catch a cold occasionally during their first two years. Colds are most contagious in the first couple of days, sometimes before the carrier knows he is sick. Therefore, it's impossible to protect your child completely from getting colds.

When Evan was three weeks old, he caught his first cold. Marlene kept a record of those days:

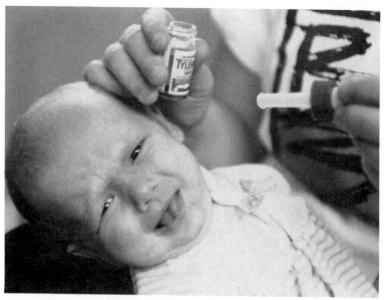

The doctor may recommend a non-aspirin pain reliever.

9/4: Today Evan has a slight cough. I hope it doesn't get worse.

9/5: Evan got the sniffles and his cough is worse. When I feed him, he'll cough, and it seems like he's choking. It scares me.

9/6: Evan's cold is getting worse. His nose is plugged. I called the doctor, and she told me to use normal saline and put it in his nose because he has a hard time breathing. I'm gonna take him to the doctor tomorrow because I want to make sure. My mom is helping me out.

9/8: Today Evan woke up around 9:00 and slept through most of the day. He's still coughing. His sniffles are getting a little better but he still gets plugged up from time to time. During the night, as usual, he's a grouch, but I finally got him to sleep by holding him in my arms and singing to him like I usually do.

9/9: Evan is a month old. He stays awake a lot. I don't mind that. It's the crying I could live without.

9/10: I wish his cold would go away. The doctor said we can't give him any medication because he's too young. I feel so sorry for him because it seems like he's having such a hard time.

9/12: He's still sick. He stays up so much, and he's always crying. I hate his cold. I don't have time these past few days to do anything because he's always awake and crying because he doesn't feel good.

9/14: Finally he's feeling better.

Neither you nor your doctor can "cure" your child's cold —there is no known cure. You can help him be more comfortable. If he has a fever or headache, Tylenol may help.

If he has a runny or stuffy nose, use normal saline and a rubber syringe to clean the discharge from baby's nose. Normal saline is available from the drugstore without a prescription. The hospital probably gave you a rubber syringe for this purpose for baby.

Decongestant medicine may also make him feel better. If his nose is sore, cream or ointment on the area is soothing.

If he's coughing, your doctor may recommend cough medicine. If he has a stuffy nose, a cold-water vaporizer will help him breathe more easily. The old-fashioned steam vaporizers are dangerous, and they don't work as well.

If he doesn't want to eat, don't worry. When he's feeling better, he'll be hungry again. Encourage him to drink juice, water, clear soups, even a little weak tea.

How often your child has a cold depends on two things: the number of people with colds to whom he is exposed, and his own resistance.

If he is in good health generally, eats nutritious meals instead of junk foods, and gets plenty of rest, he is much less likely to get sick.

He May Have an Allergy

Stuffy noses can be due to allergies. Allergies are caused generally by reactions to foods, plants, animals, or pollutants. A large percentage of allergies in children under two seem to be caused by food so doctors generally recommend changes in diet for babies with these symptoms.

A lot of allergies disappear in time as baby becomes more adjusted to life on the outside. Therefore, most doctors don't start serious allergy testing until a child is much older, usually school age.

If your baby has something like conjunctivitis (pink eye) or impetigo (skin infection), you shouldn't have him around other children. You should take the same precautions during the first day or two he has a cold.

If you know a friend's child has one of these conditions, keep your baby away from him. Of course, later when your child is out in the neighborhood playing, he will pick up an illness occasionally because you can't control your neighbor's child. These generally aren't serious diseases. Mainly they're an annoyance to both you and your child that you avoid if you can.

Keep Baby's Health Record

Keeping a family health record is important. Start with recording your baby's height and weight at birth and periodically thereafter. If you know your baby's blood type, write it down. Most important is to keep a record of your child's immunizations. You'll have to have this record when he starts to school.

Keep track of your child's illnesses. Write down the dates and briefly describe symptoms. This will help you provide information to your doctor as needed. It will also be an interesting record of this part of your child's development.

His curiosity makes him want to touch and handle everything.

He's Already Curious

Juan likes to feel and chew on things. He knows different textures, and if it's coarse, he doesn't like to hang on to it. He likes his little bunny and dog because they're soft—he puts them all over his face. Buffy (poodle) is good around him. He licks Juan's foot.

Ginny, 17 - Juan, 4 months

By four months, your baby's curiosity is growing fast, and he wants to touch and handle everything possible.

A simple face drawn on a paper plate and taped to his crib interests a newborn. No longer, however, can you give him such a flimsy thing to look at. Now his mobile must be strong enough to be hit, pulled, and abused—if he can reach it at all. And it's less frustrating to baby to have the mobile placed close enough to be touched and handled.

Delphina has a mobile of bears with music, and she grabs them. She loves sitting in a swing and watching the mobile go around.

Tiffany, 17 - Delphina, 4 months

Your baby will enjoy a well-designed mobile, preferably one he can reach and touch. This, of course, means a very sturdy mobile.

At this age, he needs a crib toy. It must be "battable" and safe. It also should make a noise—such as several rattles hanging within batting range.

Don't use something hanging from a string. Baby will get too frustrated trying to grab it and having it fly out of his reach. Think of yourself in the dark trying to turn on an old-fashioned electric bulb—the kind with the string you pull to turn it on—and the string always seems to jump out of reach. Baby will have the same problem with a toy that is not attached solidly.

An inexpensive cradle gym is a good purchase. It should have simple objects that baby can hit, pull, and handle.

Juan pulls on the handle of the cradle gym in the playpen. He pulls it down, then lets it go. He got frustrated this morning because he tried to crawl to get what he wanted, and he just couldn't do it.

Ginny

Sometime during this stage, baby will be able to reach for things he sees. This is quite different from his earlier batting at objects. Now he sees the object, reaches for it smoothly, and opens his fingers before he touches it.

An infant seat is a good purchase for this age. You can overuse it, however. Baby prefers to be carried in your arms or in a back or chest carrier rather than in a cold plastic seat. When you're working, you can put her in her infant seat near you. She'll enjoy watching you.

He Likes Mirrors

Babies love mirrors. Hold your baby in front of a full-length mirror and watch his reaction. He may be puzzled at seeing you there, apparently a second you.

His own reflection will intrigue him because he will soon learn he can make that "person" move when he moves.

I've held Kerry up to the mirror, and she looks and wonders what's going on. She's able to distinguish me from her. She knows who she is, but she isn't sure what to think of two mommies.

Leslie, 20 - Amy, 27 months; Kerry, 4 months

One of the best "toys" for this age is an unbreakable mirror placed six or seven inches from baby's eyes. Glass mirrors are dangerous. Look for a good quality plastic mirror four or five inches in diameter. If it isn't fairly good quality, his image will be distorted.

Build Trust by Responding

It's still important to respond to your baby's cries as promptly as possible. Letting him learn he can trust you to take care of his needs is not going to spoil him. Unhappy, dissatisfied, "spoiled" babies are far more likely to be babies who are already learning they can't depend on mother to come when they need her.

Jay is a good baby. He only cries when he wants something, has messy pants, or wants to eat. He does have his fussy days when he just wants to cry. Yesterday was one of those.

I barely got home from school when he started crying, and he didn't stop until 10 p.m. when he went to bed. I think he's cutting teeth. Sometimes it's hard having a baby.

Bev, 17 - Jay, 8 months

Continue to hold your baby and to rock him. Now you'll be able to do a lot more with him. This stage is usually delightful for parents.

Mark giggles and that thrills me to death. I get Bob to hurry and listen. I tickle his belly and he giggles.
Louise, 21 - Meghan, 23 months; Mark, 5 months

Throughout most of this period, baby may be happy most of the time, just as he was in the less active one-to-four-month stage. He giggles and laughs, mimics what you're doing, and generally has a wonderful time throughout much of his day. But he wants you to be nearby. If mother leaves for more than a few hours, the separation may be hard on both her and her child:

I went to the mountains for three days without Lynn, and it was hard. I couldn't really have fun because I was always thinking about her and wondering if she was all right. I knew she was being taken care of okay, but it still bothered me. When I got back, she wouldn't let me out of her sight.
Sheryl Ann, 17 - Lynn, 7 months

This doesn't mean it's wrong to take some time for yourself. It does mean you will choose carefully the person who will care for your child while you're gone. You also need to be prepared for a short period of increased dependence on you when you return.

Baby's Fears
Some babies develop other rather strong fears. Sometimes it's the vacuum cleaner. It might be the lawn mower or some other loud noise. He may decide he wants nothing to do with new places or different situations. A trip to the store may upset him.

If it's the vacuum cleaner, you could try using it while
he sleeps. A better way is to let him look and explore the
vacuum cleaner before you turn it on. Then hold him with
one arm (lovingly, *not* scoldingly) while you clean for a
few minutes. Don't overdo it, of course, but he may accept
the noise under these conditions.

Always, whatever his age, treat your child's fears as the
realities they are. It absolutely does not matter that you
know "there is nothing to be afraid of." The fact is that he
is afraid. You need to help him deal with his fear, not
scold him.

She Listens and "Talks"

By two or three months, baby will hear a sound, then
look to see where it's coming from. Sometime during this
stage, the sound of your footsteps coming toward her room
may quiet her while she watches for you. She may enjoy
soothing music, although she undoubtedly prefers the
sound of your voice singing to her.

The mirror fascinates her.

Baby is becoming much more active now. It's even more important that you talk to her, but *talk* to her, don't lecture. Hold a dialog even though she doesn't answer in words. Ask questions, then pause for her answer. That's how she learns about speech patterns. Before long she'll be responding to you with her brand of talking.

> *Carol plays with her saliva, makes sounds by spitting it out. I heard her say Da-da once, I really did. I screamed and ran to get Mario, but she hasn't done it since.*
>
> Kristyn, 17 - Carol, 3 months

Don't use "baby talk" with her. She will learn faster if she hears words pronounced correctly. Learning baby talk is not what she needs. She wants to talk like you do.

> *I talk to Gary and he goos back at me. He looks at my mouth and tries to copy my expressions and what I do with my mouth.*
>
> Leica, 18 - Gary, 4 months

> *Kerry is talked to all the time. We have two other people living here, and I take her over to my mom's about three times a week. Everybody talks to her. I like talking to her because she smiles.*
>
> Leslie

Continue Talking to Baby

Baby will begin to understand a few words during these months. He may even say "Ma-ma," "Da-da," and "Bye," but don't count on it. What you can count on is his ability to make delightful sounds. You'll hear him in his crib "talking."

This is a beautiful time to put a tape recorder by his crib. Try to turn it on just before you think he'll wake up. If you walk in to see him, however, his jabbering will stop because your face and voice are even more interesting to him than the sounds he's making himself.

Your child needs you to help him develop language. You need to talk to him and read to him long before he learns to talk himself. It's especially important now to talk about the things he knows. As you change his diaper, talk about it. As you dress him, say "Now I'm putting your shoe on your foot. Your hand goes through your sleeve." Name the parts of his body as you bathe him. Talk about the toys you're handing him.

I talk to Nick all the time. My mom talks to him and so does my dad. He's very talkative—maybe he takes after me. We've all talked to him since he was tiny. Maybe that's why he's usually happy.

Theresa, 16 - Nick, 6 months

As you carry baby around the house, show him different objects. Name and describe such things as chair, door, table, dish, picture, TV, couch. Take him outdoors and name the sidewalk, tree, fence, grass. As you do this again and again, he'll learn a lot about his world. He'll enjoy your attention, too.

Different sounds—music, an airplane, a dog barking—interest him.

Maelynn likes music—sometimes it puts her to sleep. She tries to sing along with it.

When she hears an unusual sound like an airplane, she'll stop whatever she's doing and look around to see where it's coming from. She turns around when you call her.

Joleen, 17 - Maelynn, 9 months

Sometimes when you're talking to baby, whisper in his ear. He'll enjoy the change, and he'll learn to listen to different levels of speech.

Reading Is Important

If you aren't already reading to your baby, start now.
Choose very simple stories, preferably with pictures of
things he knows. At this age, you may have trouble getting
his attention. Reading (mostly looking at pictures) at
bedtime is ideal. If baby is sleepy, he'll be more willing to
sit still for a story. If he sits or lies still long enough for a
story, he'll be more likely to go to bed without causing a lot
of commotion.

> *Carlos loves his books—he'll sit there and look at
> the books and talk to them. I told him the story of the
> Three Bears and he liked it.*
>
> Renette, 16 - Carlos, 6 months

> *I read to Jay at night after I give him his bath. It
> calms him down a little.*
>
> Bev

You don't need to buy all of baby's books. You can
make them yourself. Cut big colorful pictures out of maga-
zines. Choose pictures of things familiar to baby—a dog,
airplane, car. Pictures of babies will fascinate him. Paste
the pictures on cardboard. Punch holes in the "pages" and
tie together with brightly colored yarn.

Or you may want to invest in an inexpensive photograph
album, the kind with the plastic over the pages. The plastic
has adhesive already on it to hold the pictures in place.
After you put in the pictures and relay the plastic, tape
down all loose edges carefully with cellophane tape.

Again, choose pictures of subjects that are of particular
interest to your child.

Self-Esteem Is Crucial

Self-esteem is extremely important to all of us. Parents
must think well of themselves before they can truly think

well of their baby. To feel good about someone else, you start out by feeling good about yourself.

You can help your baby gain a good sense of self-esteem. Whenever she does something different, learns a new skill, cheer her on. If she bats at an object and manages to hit it, praise her. When she can finally grab that object, get excited with her.

> *Juan plays on the floor while I do the dishes. I'll turn to him every couple of minutes and say his name, and I think he's beginning to know it. I don't ever call him names like Fathead, because when he gets bigger, he'd believe it. When he burps, I always say, "Good boy."*
>
> Ginny

Calling a baby "Stupid" or some other put-down word can too easily turn into a "self-fulfilling prophecy."

Self-fulfilling prophecy: Something that happens because one expects it to happen.

If you tell him often enough that he's stupid, he will decide he must indeed be stupid. If he thinks he can't learn well, he probably won't. Of course you won't do that to your child.

Babies come equipped with a delightful urge to learn. Watch the baby who has just learned to turn from her back to her stomach. She will practice her new skill over and over and over again. She'll be thrilled each time she does so. Being able to do something today that she couldn't do yesterday excites her—especially if you're excited, too, and show her you are.

You have a wonderful challenge as you nurture your baby's zest for life, learning, and excitement. *Enjoy!*

At six months, he's ready for some solid food.

Good Food
For Your Baby

Your baby doesn't need—and generally shouldn't have—solid food until he is at least four or five months old. Almost all babies get along best on breast milk or formula during this time.

If you feed your baby solids too soon, he is more likely:

• to develop food allergies.

• to have digestive problems.

Feeding solids to a tiny baby is usually time-consuming and often frustrating to mother and to baby. Mother spoons it in, baby rolls it right back out! Before he's four months old, baby has a well-developed sucking reflex. He sucks before he swallows his milk. Food put in his mouth from a spoon is usually spit right back out. This is called the *protrusion reflex*.

By about four months of age, this protrusion reflex is gone, and he's much more able to accept food on his tongue. He can swallow it instead of letting it roll back out. It's as if he's saying during those early months, "Mom, I don't *want* solid food!"

They think feeding him cereal
in the evening will make him sleep
through the night—not true.

In addition, if you buy strained baby food, the cost can be rather high—high, at least, when you realize this is money spent which gives no benefit to baby during these early months. So why do so many parents start feeding cereal and other solids to their very young baby? They may have several reasons.

They may think feeding him cereal in the evening will make baby sleep through the night. Research shows this is simply not true.

Others May Urge Too-Early Solids

Sometimes people you love—perhaps your own mother—urge you to start early feeding. The research which shows that babies are better off without early solid food is fairly new. A generation or two ago, neither doctors nor the rest of us realized that early feeding can, and often does, cause allergies and stomach upsets.

When my children were babies, we thought we should start giving them cereal when they were only a few weeks old. As a result, Steve (one of my sons) has a lot of trouble with allergies. I wish I had known to delay the solid food.

Even your doctor may tell you that it's all right to start feeding solids to baby when he's very young. If this happens, talk to him/her. Some doctors seem to think all mothers want to rush solid feeding. After discussing it, you and your doctor may agree baby doesn't need cereal yet, and that it certainly is all right to wait until he's at least four months old.

If grandma is convinced that baby is starving if he drinks only milk, you (and your doctor) may decide it's important to go along with her wishes in order to avoid a family argument. Many babies can tolerate solid food by three or four months.

Holly's mother believed firmly that Orlando needed solid food by the time he was a month old, and she insisted that Holly feed him cereal and fruit. Holly resisted her advice for awhile:

I breastfed Orlando completely. I knew he didn't need anything else. When he was a month old, my mother started telling me I should give him some solid food. Mom is a nurse and worked with the newborns at the hospital several years ago. She thinks she knows exactly what to do with every baby, especially Orlando.

She kept telling me he wasn't gaining enough weight. She was surprised when the doctor weighed him and said he was just fine. Mom still thought I was starving him.

To make matters worse, I made the mistake of quoting the nurse at school. That really upset her. I guess she thought I was going over her head or something.

When Orlando was about 2 1/2 months old, I decided it wasn't worth the hassle. And the nurse at school agreed with me. A little cereal and strained fruit each day would hurt Orlando less than the fussing between Mom and me.

Holly, 17 - Orlando, 5 months

You need to know that ideally your baby should have only breast milk or formula for four to six months. You also need to consider your reality as Holly did, then make your decision.

Solids by Six Months

Ideally, then, you don't feed baby solid food for at least four months. It's important, however, that you *do* start spoonfeeding her and giving her finger foods by the time she's six months old. Reasons to feed solid food to baby by six months include:

- She needs nutrients she isn't getting from breast milk or formula.
- She needs to learn to eat solids, a quite different process from getting her food through sucking.

Four to six months seems to be the ideal age to help baby learn this new method of eating. It's also important by this time that she learn to eat a variety of foods.

I waited about five months to give Nick solid foods. He likes to be nursed after he eats, and then he falls asleep. I used to leak, and I wanted to nurse him, but I think it's best to feed him solids first. I give him cereal in the morning, then bring him here to the center where I nurse him.

Theresa, 16 - Nick, 6 months

Rice Cereal First

Start with infant rice cereal. Use the dry, iron-enriched kind that you buy in a box. Rice is less likely to cause allergies than other kinds of cereal such as wheat. Above all, please don't start with the mixed cereal. If she's allergic to just one of the ingredients, you won't know which one it is.

Mix the dry rice cereal with a little formula. If you're breastfeeding, you can pump enough milk for her cereal at first. She'll be more willing to accept the cereal if it smells and tastes somewhat like her formula or breast milk. Mix enough milk with the cereal to make it quite thin at first.

Carefully choose the "right" time for teaching baby to eat solid food. Don't attempt spoon-feeding at first when she's terribly hungry. She would be furious at the delay in getting the bottle or breast she wants.

She needs to be reasonably hungry or she won't bother trying this new food. About half-through her breast or bottle feeding is the best time.

A small, narrow, shallow-bowled spoon with a fairly long handle works best for these early feedings. To baby, eating from a regular teaspoon feels like eating from a huge tablespoon would feel to us. (Try it sometime. You'll see

why she needs a little spoon to match her mouth size.)

If baby doesn't sit up by herself yet, put her in your lap or in her infant seat for her first solid food experience. She needs to be a little more upright than for her breast or bottle feeding.

She prefers feeding herself.

Next step is for you to relax! If she doesn't like cereal the first time, that's okay. Try again tomorrow—and the next day. If she still resists, wait a few days before trying again. If she swallows a bit of cereal, congratulate her. Be thrilled—show her you're pleased. If she doesn't eat it, don't make a big deal of it.

Warning

Sometimes parents mix cereal and formula together, then feed it to baby from a bottle. *Don't!* Your baby needs to learn to eat from a spoon.

An infant feeder which practically "injects" the food into her mouth is bad too. *Don't buy it.*

Let her drink milk and water from a bottle. Help her learn that solid foods are eaten from a spoon. Fairly soon she will also learn about finger foods.

Vegetables, Fruits for Baby

Start feeding baby vegetables, fruits, and their juices sometime between his fifth and seventh months. Traditionally, babies have eaten white fruits first, usually applesauce or pears, perhaps because almost all babies like the taste. After the sweet taste of fruit, however, baby may balk at vegetables. You may decide to start with a vegetable— perhaps squash, sweet potatoes, or carrots.

Mashed banana is often one of the first foods given to baby. Most babies like it, and it's super-easy to mash to a smooth consistency.

At first, offer baby only one new food each week. If he's allergic to that food—if he gets a rash or seems to have a digestion problem—you'll know that particular food is probably causing the problem. If you fed him a new food each day, you wouldn't have any idea which one to remove.

Your baby can probably:

• Hold and gum a teething biscuit by 5 months.

• Handle little pieces of hard-boiled egg yolk (no egg white yet) by 6 months.

• Eat dry unsugared cereal, soft toast, French toast, cooked carrot and potato pieces, peas with skins broken, even diced liverwurst sandwiches by 7 months.

He can handle all these things himself by eating with his fingers.

By the time he's eight months old, you'll be able to mash his food into small pieces. If you're serving chicken, get rid of the bone and cartilage. Then cut the meat into very small pieces for him.

Fish is excellent because it just falls apart. Of course, you have to be very careful to get all the bones out first.

Warning

Orange juice is not recommended until baby is about a year old. Some babies are allergic to it.

Many babies like cottage cheese. Just mash it with a fork.

Plain unflavored yogurt is good for baby. Don't choose the heavily sugared kind. Many children prefer the tart flavor of plain yogurt.

The above foods, along with formula or breast milk, can supply most of baby's vitamin and mineral needs. Iron-fortified cereal can satisfy her need for iron. Fruits and vegetables, of course, are good sources of vitamins A and C. Your doctor may also want baby to continue taking her vitamin drops.

Drinking from a Cup

When she's five or six months old, offer baby a little
milk or juice in a cup. You can buy a cup with a lid and a
spout as a bridge between bottle and cup. Before long,
she'll be able to drink a little milk, water and juice from
her cup.

*Nick is learning to drink from a cup. Yesterday I
gave him a training cup, and he's learning how to use
it. He eats flour tortillas. He eats crackers and holds
them himself.*

Theresa, 16 - Nick, 6 months

*I'm trying to give Orlando a bottle occasionally,
but he doesn't want one. He does good already with a
cup. He holds on to it, and he can take it right to his
mouth although his coordination isn't very good yet.*

Holly, 17 - Orlando, 5 months

If you're still breastfeeding her, you may decide to wean
her directly to a cup in the next three or four months. If you
haven't used bottles much, weaning will probably be easier
for you if you let her go from your breast to the cup. Some
babies are ready to drink enough milk from a cup by their
first birthday. Others need to breastfeed a little longer.

If she's bottle-fed, she still needs to learn to drink from a
cup. She'll spill it, even try pouring it out if you give her
too much. With patience, she'll learn. Remember, she
needs about 20 ounces of milk daily, whether by cup
or bottle.

When He Feeds Himself

*He's trying hard to use the spoon—doesn't quite have
it yet. He puts his food on his spoon, but has trouble
getting it to his mouth.*

Arlene, 17 - Dale, 11 months

If baby wants to help feed himself, let him. He won't be able to get much food to his mouth at first. He can put his hand on yours as you hold the spoon. Or he can have his own spoon while you get most of the food to his mouth with yours.

When she's eating, she likes to get the spoon and bang it for awhile, then eat for awhile, then bang it again. She doesn't like me to feed her unless she's in a good mood. She likes to feed herself. She drinks by herself from a training cup although she still takes a bottle.

Joleen, 17 - Maelynn, 9 months

Give him finger foods as early as he can handle them. By the time he's six or seven months old, he can pick up small slices of banana or Cheerios. Before long he'll be ready for graham crackers, pieces of toast, teething biscuits, even little bits of meat and cheese.

Alice won't eat out of a spoon. She refuses. She'll pick it up and eat it with her fingers. She doesn't eat a lot because I guess she's attached to the milk.

First I fed her fruits, bananas and applesauce. Then at eight months she went to regular food. String beans are her favorite.

She eats any kind of meat herself—turkey, chicken, anything. She has ten teeth. She can chew the bone from the chicken wing without my cutting off the meat.

Melanie, 15 - Alice 13 months

Cheerios are a marvelous early food-toy. He'll pick one up in each hand, look at it, stick it in his mouth. They contain some nutrition and, most important, are very low in sugar.

Don't give him sugar cereals. Such "cereals" should be labeled breakfast candy. Some are actually more than half sugar!

Sometimes people try to pacify a child with a sweet treat when a hug would work just as well. In fact, hugs are always better than junk food. Jello water and other sweetened drinks are in the empty calorie category too. Babies and toddlers need milk, water and unsweetened fruit juices to drink—and seldom anything else.

Coffee, tea, and cola drinks contain caffeine which is a drug. Your baby doesn't need drugs.

He's Messy!

Sonja bangs her cracker on the table and it smears all over and flies everywhere!

Julie, 16 - Sonja, 7 months

Are you a fairly neat person? If so, don't expect baby to follow your example. A baby learning to feed himself is at his messiest. Don't be shocked. Expect it and be prepared to cope with it.

Gilbert likes to feed himself, and he makes the biggest mess. He eats mashed potatoes and string beans. He has six teeth, and he can even chew on meat already.

Gaye, 15 - Gilbert, 7 months

The easiest way to feed him is to put him in a sturdy high chair. When he starts feeding himself, lay newspapers under the chair. A piece of heavy plastic protecting your floor might look better than newspaper, but you don't want something you have to clean.

After each meal, just bundle up the newspapers and throw them out.

Dale is on table food. He doesn't much like eating meat, but he likes vegetables. I don't have to mash them—if I do, he gets mad because he can't pick them up. He gets mad if I try to feed him, too, so I just put food on his tray.

Arlene, 17 - Dale, 11 months

Remember how much baby likes to explore, to touch, to feel? That's exactly what he will do with his food. Some of it will go in his mouth, but at first more seems to end up on his face, in his hair, any place but where you'd like it to go. He will be delighted with the whole mess.

When he wants to help, give him bits of toast or banana to hold while you feed him. He may get some food to his mouth by smearing it there with his palm. Looking at, handling, tasting and smelling food is part of the same exploring that begins earlier with inedibles. If he's allowed to work out his own eating habits, he learns the world is not a restrictive forbidding place where showing his own feelings and wants only brings trouble.

Keep cool and go along with his sheer enjoyment of the whole eating process. This is the best route to making his mealtimes the pleasant events you want them to be.

Eating takes lots of concentration at this stage.

Preparing Food
For Your Baby

*J*uan *has cereal and fruit for breakfast, fruit and
vegetables at noon, fruit and vegetables at night. The
doctor is starting him on beef and lamb mixed with
vegetables. He doesn't like the dry cereal so he eats
the kind in the jar mixed with fruit. I don't know how
to fix baby food myself.*

Ginny, 17 - Juan, 5 months

That's a lot of little jars of food that Juan eats every day.
Many people buy ready-prepared strained baby food. Either
they don't know how to fix it at home, or they feel they
don't have time to prepare it.

Do you realize you don't have to buy those jars? You
can easily fix baby's food yourself.

There are two big advantages to preparing baby food
at home:

First, it's cheaper to buy a carrot and cook and mash it than to pay 36¢-50¢ for a 4.5 ounce jar of strained carrots. When you're tempted to start buying prepared baby food, check the prices in your store.

Do a little arithmetic. How much would it cost each week or each month to buy several jars of baby food every day? Wouldn't you rather have some new clothes for yourself or for baby? Or money for furniture or a night out?

Second, and even more important, is nutritive value. You won't be using fillers to stretch the amount of food. You won't be adding salt and sugar that baby doesn't need. You'll know exactly what your baby is getting.

If you decide to buy strained baby food, read the labels carefully before you buy:

- Choose basic fruits, vegetables, and strained meats.

- Don't buy combination meals because you get less protein per serving with them than you would if you mixed together a jar of meat and a jar of vegetables yourself.

- If the label tells you the food contains a lot of sugar and modified starches, don't buy it.

- Skip the baby desserts because baby doesn't need them any more than the rest of us do.

Cooked Fruit

- Wash, peel, and cut apples, peaches, pears, plums, or apricots into small pieces. Remove pits.

- Simmer or steam until tender (10-20 minutes). Don't add sugar.

- Using baby food grinder or blender, blend until smooth.

You Can Fix It Yourself

Fixing food for baby is easy. If you have a blender, use it. Or you can buy a baby food grinder for just a few dollars. With it, you prepare small amounts of food for baby. The blender is easier for fixing larger amounts.

You need nothing but a fork and a saucer to mash a banana. Choose a ripe banana, one that's yellow with brown spots on the peel. If, after you mash it, it seems a bit thick for baby, mix it with a little milk.

It might take 40 seconds longer to mash a banana than it would to open a jar of strained banana. It's certainly cheaper than buying the banana in the jar. You can fix half a banana, cover the other half and refrigerate it. It will keep for two days.

Important vitamins are lost when you cook foods in boiling water. The steam method of cooking will save more of those vitamins. The food is held above the boiling water so it will cook only in the steam.

A steam basket, available in most department stores, fits into most pans. You need to use a pan with a tight-fitting lid. Many adults prefer steamed vegetables because foods cooked this way retain more natural flavor.

If you have a microwave oven, you may prefer to cook baby's food there. Follow the directions that came with

Cooked Vegetables

- Simmer cut-up vegetables in 1 inch of water or steam over boiling water until tender.

- Mash or blend the vegetables.

- Add cooking water to get the right consistency.

your oven. Cooking time will vary depending on the
amount you cook and the power of your microwave.

If you're cooking for the whole family, be sure to take
baby's portion out *before* you add salt, sugar, and other
seasonings. She won't mind. A craving for extra salt is
learned by eating foods with added salt. Don't season her
food to meet your taste. You're fixing it for your baby, not
yourself.

Too much salt in one's diet can cause numerous health
problems including hypertension. Eating sugar may cause a
craving for sweets. Help your baby avoid these problems
by having as little salt and sugar as possible in her diet.

Finding Time to Fix It

Many mothers say they don't fix baby food at home
because they don't have time. If you're working full-time
or going to school, or if you have other children, of course
you're busy. Most of us will agree that one baby keeps a
mother overly busy. So how can you find time for all this
blending and grinding of baby food?

If possible, use your family's meals as a start. If you're
having a vegetable, put a small amount (without seasonings) through a baby food grinder. Perhaps you're having a

Meat for Baby

• Use meat you've cooked for your family.

• Blend to a smooth consistency.

• Add a little water, broth, or juice as needed.

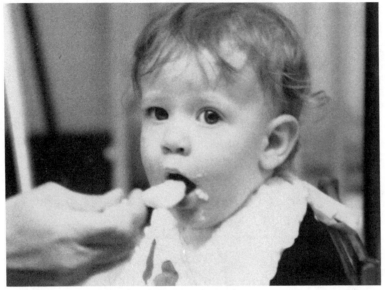

Eating is serious business.

meat that is also suitable for blending. Do you like applesauce? If so, share it with baby.

> *I broil hamburger and put it in the blender with a little bit of milk. When we have chicken for dinner, I put it in the blender, or I give her the drumstick to chew on.*
>
> Julie, 16 - Sonja, 7 months

If your family meals aren't suitable for baby, you can still prepare her food without spending several hours each day. Best approach is to cook and freeze ahead. If you spend a Saturday morning preparing baby food, you can be set for a month. Or invite another mother over and have a cooking-for-baby party one evening.

Unless you know exactly what and how you want to cook, investing in a baby food cookbook would help. My favorite is Vicki Lansky's *Feed Me—I'm Yours* (Meadowbrook Press). It's available at most book stores.

Ms. Lansky describes two methods of freezing baby food. For the food cube method, you simply pour prepared food into ice cube trays. Freeze it quickly. Then store the cubes in plastic freezer bags or in reusable containers. Be sure to label and date the food you're freezing. Use it within two months.

To freeze baby food by Ms. Lansky's "plop" method, "plop" it by spoonfuls onto a cookie sheet. "Plop" the amount you think baby will eat at one meal. Freeze quickly, remove from cookie sheet, and put in plastic freezer bags.

She suggests you keep protein food, cereals, vegetables, and fruits in separate containers in the freezer.

> *Baby will need strained food*
> *for only a couple of months.*

When you're ready to serve the cubes or "plops" of food, thaw in a warming dish or in an egg-poaching cup over boiling water. The little individual egg-poaching pan is a convenient size and is relatively inexpensive.

You don't need to warm the food beyond room temperature. Baby's taste buds are not fully developed, and what seems warm to you may seem hot to baby.

Small amounts of frozen baby food are handy for short

Uncooked Fruit

• Wash and peel an apple, pear, peach, or apricot.

• Add a little water.

• Blend.

• **NOTE: Offer after six months of age.**

trips. By the time you arrive at your friend's house, baby's food will probably be thawed and ready to serve.

With a little planning, you can have a nice variety of food stored in your freezer. If you fix a different vegetable for your family each night one week, simply cook at least twice the amount you need. Prepare the extra amount for baby, then freeze. Do the same with fruits. You may find it easier than running to the store to buy jars of baby food.

If you wait until he's six months old to start baby on solid food, you'll need to use strained food for only a couple of months. He can be eating table food, much of it mashed, by the time he's eight months old.

Even if you don't want to prepare strained baby food yourself, you surely won't buy jars of junior food. Feeding him from the family meals is so little bother to you, and it's better for baby.

—Not the First Year—

Raw, crisp fruits and vegetables aren't good for baby until past the first year because he might choke on them. Until he's two, in fact, if you want him to have raw carrots, you should grate them.

Corn is not for infants or toddlers. It goes right through in the BM without changing color or shape.

Now is the time to help your baby grow into a pattern of healthy eating that will continue throughout his life. Feeding him a variety of foods gives him an opportunity to develop a taste for different foods.

You'll do him a real favor if you delay giving him junk food—soda, candy, chips, etc.—as long as possible. Your job is to help him learn to enjoy eating the food he needs to grow into a healthy, capable adult.

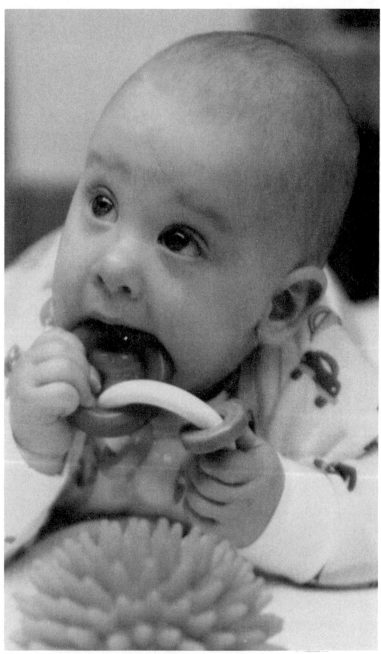

Watch out! Soon he'll be crawling everywhere.

Your Baby
Is on the Move

*Now at five months, Orlando is more alert, more a
person. When he was little, he just lay there and
really couldn't see me clearly. Now he rolls over,
coos, growls (really!), plays with his feet and his
hands, and laughs.*

*When he was a newborn I held him a lot, and he
loved that. Now, I hold him and play with him. I
spend about as much time playing with him now as I
did holding him, perhaps a little more. He's teething
and is a little fussy.*

Holly, 17 - Orlando, 5 months

Five-month-old Sara stays pretty much where you put
her. Lay her on a blanket with a few toys. Go back ten
minutes later and she's in the same general area. She may
be able to dig her toes in and scoot a little. She can turn

from her back to her stomach and back again. But she's not
moving all over the apartment yet.

Nine-month-old Sam is an entirely different being. Lay
him on a blanket on the floor, turn your back for a second,
and he's across the room! He may be learning to crawl.
The physical changes happening between five and nine
months in a baby's life are startling. Until he's four or five
months old, baby is limited to lying on his back or his
stomach or being propped up by someone else. He depends
completely on others to move him from place to place.

Sitting—Standing—Crawling

By about 61/2 months, many babies sit up by themselves.
Many start creeping or crawling about a month later. But,
as in every kind of development, each child is different.
Don't worry if your baby isn't sitting up or crawling
quite yet.

> *Nick sits up by himself for a long time, then he
> collapses. Then I set him up again. When he gets
> tired, he lies down. He entertains himself for a longer
> time now.*
>
> Theresa, 16 - Nick, 6 months

> *Wayne's been crawling since seven months, but he
> didn't sit up until about that time. I like the crawling
> because now he can do something.*
>
> Erin, 23 - Wayne, 9 months; Kelton, 7 years

The age at which she sits up, crawls, and walks seems to
have nothing to do with her I.Q. when she's older. The
baby who doesn't move off the blanket during much of her
first year may be one of the brightest kids around.

To some parents, baby's intellectual development is very
important. There are many kinds of intelligence. One child
may be very interested in learning pre-reading skills;

another may be fascinated with insects and spend lots of time watching them move. Perhaps your child can hardly wait for an opportunity to help mom or dad fix things around the house.

The child who doesn't read well in kindergarten may be repairing the family car a few years later, a task her reading brother may find impossible.

Remember that your child, whatever his abilities, is important; your child is a fun person. Enjoy him. Whether or not he is "brilliant" is not terribly important.

Sometime toward the end of this five-to-nine-month period, your baby may pull herself to a standing position. She'll hang on for dear life to her crib railing or to the arm of the couch. At first she's pleased, but in a minute she may start crying—she doesn't know how to sit down again!

You can help her learn to sit down. Show her how. Gently bend her knees as you talk to her. She'll sit down— and two minutes later she's up again. It may take several days for her to learn to get down by herself.

She loves to play on the floor with mom.

Curiosity Leads to Crawling

As baby lies on the floor or sits in his infant seat, his curiosity is building rapidly.

Put yourself in his place. Imagine what it must be like not to be able to move. You see all those exciting things around you, and all you can do is look at them. Imagine the frustration!

Wanting to satisfy his curiosity is baby's biggest reason for learning to crawl. He likes the exercise and being able to move his body, but satisfying his curiosity is the big incentive.

> *This past couple of weeks Jonita has started pulling herself up on the chair. She likes to stand and doesn't like to sit very often. This morning my sister got her up and set her in the living room. She went in the bedroom, and when she came out, Jonita was clear across the room!*
>
> Ellen, 17 - Jonita, 6 months

Before they walk, babies get around in a variety of ways. Classic crawling is getting up on his hands and knees and moving around. Some babies pull themselves along on their tummies. Others stand up on their feet and hands, then "walk" like a little puppy. Whichever method your baby chooses, he is delighted that he can finally get around.

Did you know that baby needs your help to learn to crawl? No, you don't need to show her how to move her legs and arms. It *is* important that you give her lots of opportunity to move around. That means not caging her in a playpen or setting her in her highchair or in a walker for long periods of time.

Instead, put her on the floor on a blanket. Dress her so she won't hurt her knees and let her go. And before you know it, she will go—all over the house! Of course, you need to baby-proof your home by this time.

*When Lynn started crawling, I couldn't sit around
any longer and not watch her when she was on the
floor. She's going all the time—and so am I!*

> Sheryl Ann, 17 - Lynn, 7 months

*Clark didn't crawl two weeks ago, but now he
speeds all over the place. What a change!*

> Kathleen, 18 - Clark, 7 months, and Aaron, 2 years

Baby Learning

She's beginning to see that she can make things happen.
Let her flip the light on and off. When she realizes she can
make the light go on, then off again, she'll be delighted.
She may want to continue practicing this magic for
several minutes.

Jay is learning he can make something happen. After
awhile he'll realize that if he does one thing, something
else will occur. He has discovered cause and effect:

*Jay knows how to work a light switch now. I'll put
him by one, and he'll make it go on and off. At first he
didn't know he was turning the light on and off. I
said, "Look," and he paid attention. He was thrilled.*

> Bev, 17 - Jay, 8 months

Maelynn is learning rapidly. She's even using "tools" to
get what she wants:

*My mom has sheets over the sofa. When Maelynn
wants something up there that she can't reach, she
will pull on the sheet until she can get it.*

> Joleen, 17 - Maelynn, 9 months

First Physics Lesson

Along about this time, while she's sitting in her
highchair, baby will have her first physics lesson. She'll
drop a spoon or a toy to the floor, then lean over to see

He examines everything he can reach.

what happened to it. This is serious learning on her part, and she'll try it again and again.

Of course mother or dad is supposed to hand the item back to her. Parents vary as to how long they're willing to continue this game. Most, however, will go along with it for awhile, especially when they realize it's a learning time for baby.

You can tie some toys to the high chair with a heavy string. Baby will learn to pull it back up herself. At first she won't be able to do that. She needs you to do it for her.

Robin drops something from her high chair, watches it drop, then screams for me to pick it up. Then I tie it on a string so she doesn't hear it hit the floor. Now she's learning to pick it up with the string.

Melinda

Time for Teeth

The "average" baby (yours may be quite different) cuts her first teeth when she is six or seven months old. She will probably get her lower incisors first. By eight or nine months, she may have four of her upper teeth.

Some babies fuss when their teeth are cutting through their gums. Others seem to notice very little, if any, discomfort. One mother reported she knew her child had cut his teeth when she heard the spoon clanking against the tooth.

> *When Dale was teething, I didn't even know he was. He would be cranky once in awhile, but I just thought he was tired or something.*
>
> Arlene, 17 - Dale, 11 months

For some babies, teething is a painful experience. She may want to bite everything in sight. Give her a teething ring. Store several in the freezer. If the ring is cold, she'll like it better.

Try freezing thin slices of cantaloupe for your teething baby. Of course you carefully remove all seeds and rind from the melon. Baby can suck on the frozen piece and, when it thaws, gum it and swallow it.

> *Jay has a tooth that's not all the way in. He's keeping me up for hours. Nothing seems to work. I put teething lotion on it, whiskey, ice cubes, but nothing helps.*
>
> Bev

You can buy teething lotion which may help soothe painful gums. Put it on baby's gums a few minutes before feeding time. It may take away some of the pain so that she can eat more comfortably.

Baby may drool while she's teething. If so, put a terrycloth bib on her.

These first teeth are not chewing teeth. They won't help much when she's trying to chew food. She'll still have to

gum solid food with lumps in it. But she may try to chew
the nipple on her bottle.

If you're breastfeeding, she may try biting your nipple.
If the nipple is well back in her mouth as it should be for
sucking, she can't bite. The only problem is when she stops
sucking and decides to play.

If she bites, remove your nipple from her mouth with a
firm "No." Pause for a few seconds even if she's whimper-
ing because you've taken her food away. Then if she wants
to eat, let her. But don't let her bite you. Many breastfed
babies learn not to bite after only a few days of this
approach.

If your baby gets a fever, don't blame it on teething. She
may fuss, she may even have a tiny bit of fever if her teeth
are bothering her. But if she has a "real" fever (higher than
101^0), she's sick. A fever indicates an infection. Call your
doctor.

Guard against cavities in those little teeth from the
beginning. Encourage her to drink water. It's certainly
better for her teeth than are sweet drinks, and water helps
rinse milk and other foods out of her mouth.

Avoid sweet foods. During this period you should be
able to keep candy and other sweets almost entirely away
from baby. If she doesn't know about them, she won't cry
for junk foods. The same suggestion applies to soda and
other soft drinks. Don't even give her a taste. Her teeth will
thank you.

Nursing Bottle Syndrome

Even a bottle of milk can be a problem for baby's teeth.
True, her teeth need a lot of calcium in order to develop
properly and to stay healthy. The best source of calcium
is milk. She needs about 20 ounces of milk each day at
this stage.

A bottle of milk is a problem if she keeps the bottle nipple in her mouth as she falls asleep, and it stays there. Milk dribbling into her mouth during the night keeps her teeth covered with a film of milk. Milk, nutritious as it is, has enough natural sugar in it to damage teeth if it stays there hour after hour.

Dentists see so many toddlers with rotten little teeth in front that they have given this condition a name: Nursing Bottle Syndrome.

The solution, if baby wants a bottle in bed with her, is to fill the bottle with water. Fruit juice is even worse than milk because it has more sugar in it. If she needs the sucking when she goes to sleep, she can get it with a bottle filled with water or with a pacifier.

Taking a bottle of milk to bed can become a very strong habit, a habit that is hard to change. Perhaps you can hold her while she drinks her bottle of milk. When she's big enough to take the bottle to bed with her, always put water in it. Then she won't risk having Nursing Bottle Syndrome.

Tremendous Changes Already!

Your pre-toddler has changed tremendously in these first nine months. As she scoots across the floor, you may think she's into everything already. But amazingly soon she will be walking, then running. Keeping up with her will be— already is—an exciting challenge. *Are you ready?*

Being with mom (or dad) is where she wants to be.

Playing with Your Baby

What I like about him is he's fun. He's real playful with almost everybody. You play with him just a little bit and he'll smile a lot. He always has a smile on his face. People say he looks like me.

I like taking him with me to the park when I go there with my friends to play handball. There are 4 or 5 of my friends at my house every day. They help me out a lot.

Andy, 17 - Gus, 5 months (Yolanda, 15)

Simple Toys Are Best

Your little pre-walker may often play alone for as long as an hour—if mother or dad is nearby. Talk to her as you work. Give her a different object to play with every once in awhile.

Collect small objects for your child to play with and to explore. Let her spend a lot of time on the floor on a blanket. In front of her, put several small items and a container for them. Choose things that are two to five inches in size and with a variety of shapes and textures. She'll spend a lot of time exploring these objects and practicing simple skills with them.

These small objects don't need to be expensive toys. She'll undoubtedly prefer items from your kitchen drawers. For example:

- Plastic measuring spoons and cups

- Shiny can of sardines

- Plastic freezer container

- Big pan

Put everything in the big pan, and she'll be delighted. She'll look at each thing as she takes it out of the pan. She'll feel it and chew it. She may bang things together.

Be sure the items you offer her are safe. The handle on a wooden spoon or even some pan handles can be dangerous if she falls on them.

When she's tired of these things, you'll find more in your kitchen. Just be sure each thing you give her is smooth and safe for her. Nothing should be smaller than 1 1/2 inches. Remember, anything you give her will be mouthed if at all possible.

Nick likes the Playtex bottle and other containers. I cleaned out one container and put little rocks in it, and he loves that. Of course I taped the lid on tight.
                                              Theresa, 16 - Nick, 6 months

Sometime during this stage, baby will be ready for simple stacking toys. You can give her plastic cups that will nest. Be sure they don't stick together.

Time for Games

Even though baby can now play alone, give him attention when he's happily occupied as well as when he's fussing. As he plays, talk to him, throw him a kiss, hug him as you walk by. Smiling often at him will be easy.

He'll love to play games with you. Give him a few minutes of your time several times a day for games.

Playtime

Hide-and-seek can change. He may hide behind a chair and ask you to find him. He'll go into gales of giggling as you look behind each chair until you "find" the right one.

Maelynn likes to play choo-choo. She does it herself sometimes. When she's in the walker, she'll go behind something, then look out at me to surprise me, and I'll laugh.

She was trying to make me laugh the other day— she bumped her head lightly on the padded headboard. She didn't get hurt, and I laughed. So she did it again to make me laugh again.

Joleen, 17 - Maelynn, 9 months

Get on his level. Play on the floor with him when he learns to crawl. He'll love having you chase him all around the living room floor. Soon he may decide to chase you instead.

Sonja loves to play peek-a-boo. My mom says to play it with her a lot because it's like me disappearing and then coming back. She'll hold covers over her face, then drop them. I'll say "Boo!" and she'll laugh. Or we'll play peek-a-boo around the corner.

Julie, 16 - Sonja, 7 months

Making Toys

Rice bags. Make him some small rice bags and show him how to throw them. Use a different textured fabric for each little bag—fur, satin, corduroy, and vinyl, for example. Simply cut two circles of fabric for each rice bag. With right sides together, sew tightly (preferably on a sewing machine) around the edge leaving a one-inch space for turning and stuffing. Turn right side out. Fill with rice. Sew up the hole with tiny stitches.

Using rice to stuff these little bags is far safer than using beans. He could choke on a bean. He could have a real problem if he stuffed a bean in his ear or nose. Don't risk it.

Feel-box. Use a box for the container. Put in a linoleum square, a playing card, big rubber sink stopper, and squares of different kinds of textured fabric.

Coffee can/clothes pins toy. You can make a fine toy using a one-pound coffee can and the old-fashioned non-spring clothespins. Make sure the edge of the coffee can is smooth. Simply set the clothespins on the edge of the can. You might want to use a non-toxic paint to paint them red, yellow, and blue. You don't expect him to learn his colors yet, but you begin to introduce the idea of color when you say, "Let's put the red one on the can."

Drop the spool in the hole. A coffee can with a plastic lid can also be used for a "drop the spool in the hole" game. Cut a hole in the plastic coffee can lid a little bigger than the spools. Then show baby how to drop the spools into the can. Lids from frozen juice containers also work well as the drop-in toy.

They're checking each other out.

Maelynn likes to play with her beach ball and a little tennis ball. She throws it, then wants someone to bring it back again.

Joleen, 17 - Maelynn, 9 months

Balls are the best toy of all for baby. He can roll them and throw them. Once he can crawl, he can go after the ball. Soon he'll enjoy a big beach ball as well as having a wonderful time with the smaller ones. Of course he likes it best if you play with him:

We sit on the floor and I roll the ball to Sonja. She can't roll it back yet, but she laughs.

Julie, 16 - Sonja, 7 months

A small metal pan with a lid is a great toy. It takes patience and skill for baby to fit the lid on the pan. If you put a small object inside for a surprise, he'll be even more interested. After he has carefully examined the pan, you may need to show him how to take the lid off and put it back on.

You can also show him how a block sounds when you hit the pan with it. Show him the different sounds it makes when you tap his shoe with the block, then the floor. Noise is an important part of baby's life.

Sonja bangs everything. She loves to make noise. She wakes up at 5 or 6 a.m. and screams—not crying, just noisy.

                                                                    Julie

Robin takes cans and rolls them down the floor. She bangs toys all the time. The other morning she got up and crawled into the kitchen, opened the door—and I heard all the pans fall out. Then she screamed because it scared her.

                                        Melinda, 15 - Robin, 9 months

Playtime

Make a game out of baby learning to use one thing to get another. Sit on the floor with your baby. Put a small blanket in front of him. Put a toy on the blanket, but out of your child's reach. Show your child how to get the toy by pulling on the blanket.

Can he do it himself?

Baby will enjoy going outdoors with you. If he isn't crawling yet, lay him on a blanket near you while you work in your yard. When he starts crawling, let him play in the grass. A little dirt won't hurt him. You need to watch him rather closely, of course.

Sunshine is lovely and provides some vitamin D for your child if his skin is exposed to it. Too much sunshine is harmful. Babies should have very limited doses. Start out with two minutes of sun a day, front and back. Don't expose baby to midday sun in the hot summer. Sunning sessions should be before 10 a.m. and after 3 p.m. Be sure to protect your baby's eyes from the sun.

If you take your baby or toddler to the beach, you'll need an umbrella unless you're staying for only a few minutes.

Water Play

Babies love water play. It can be relaxing for them, too. If you can't put baby outside with some water, perhaps you can arrange it in your kitchen without too much trouble.

First, put down a good padding of newspapers, then spread an old sheet over them. Put some water in a plastic dish. One or two inches of water is enough—you want him to splash, not flood the place.

You'll find he first splashes the water, tastes it, and has a good time finding out all he can about it. You can add to his fun by giving him a couple of ice cubes. Take them out when they get so small he could choke if he put them in his mouth. You can even put a little food coloring in the water.

When baby can sit up by himself, you'll probably bathe him in the big bathtub. He'll love having a few floating toys with him. Tell him to wash the fish's hair while you wash his.

A plastic sieve for water play can be made from the lower half of a plastic milk jug. Just poke holes in it with an ice pick.

Make him a bath mitt with a washcloth. Cut two pieces of cloth the shape and size of baby's hand. Sew them together and, if you like, decorate them. Let him help wash himself with his mitten. Of course you'll never turn your back on him for a second while he's in the water.

Walkers? Playpens?

During the early part of this stage, your child may still use her infant seat. Place her in the seat near you so she can watch you work. Be sure you set her in a safe place on the floor. As soon as she can sit up by herself, however, she won't want to sit in it. By that time, she probably would not be safe in it, either. She might be able to tip it over.

Unless he's sitting straight up, Carlos bounces right out of his infant seat. If he's not doing it by himself, you might as well forget it.
                                        Renette, 16 - Carlos, 6 months

Many families purchase a walker for their baby. This is fine if you're going to supervise her closely. A walker is a crutch which lets a child get around before she can do so by herself. She may go into dangerous areas, or pull things down onto herself. So watch her! And don't leave her in the walker for a long time. She's better off on the floor.

We don't have a playpen. I'd rather put Maelynn in a walker and let her do whatever she wants. She moves around, but only when she's really interested in something. She isn't getting into things yet from crawling, but she does when she's in a walker.
I put her in the walker and open the cupboards and let her get stuff out to play.
                                        Joleen

Robin jumps up and down in her walker and runs around. It's good except it gives her too much support front and back. She won't want to learn to walk if she's in it too long.
                                        Melinda, 15 - Robin, 9 months

Playpens are also used by many families. If you take a poll on your street, you'll probably find several babies caged in playpens. In fact, some babies put up with spending several hours a day in a playpen.

A playpen is a handy item to take to the beach. A seven-month-old baby is not ready to be turned loose in the sand.

At home, the playpen can be a safe and fun place for a baby for perhaps ten minutes—long enough for you to take a shower.

> *Playpens are all right, but not for a long period of time. I would feel caged in if I had that little area. But when I'm cleaning the house, sometimes I put Sonja in there for a little while. It gets hard trying to do something now that she goes everywhere.*
>
> *When she's playing in her playpen and she gets restless, I put that picture of me right outside her playpen. Sonja looks at it and gets quiet. My sister started that, and it was a great idea. Or I put a big mirror outside the playpen.*

Julie

But babies generally are bored in playpens. Some scream until you let them out. Others may not fuss so much, especially if they have been stuck in their pen since they were tiny.

But how much do you learn when you're bored? Not much! Your bored baby doesn't learn much either. If you use a playpen, do so as little as possible. Your baby needs to be able to satisfy her curiosity.

She will learn so much more playing with you, being near you as you work, than she possibly could learn off by herself in a playpen. Arranging her environment so she can have freedom to explore is part of your job as a parent. Baby will appreciate your efforts.

See *Teens Parenting—Discipline from Birth to Three* for suggestions on baby-proofing your house so you and baby can survive her creeping/toddling months with as little frustration as possible.

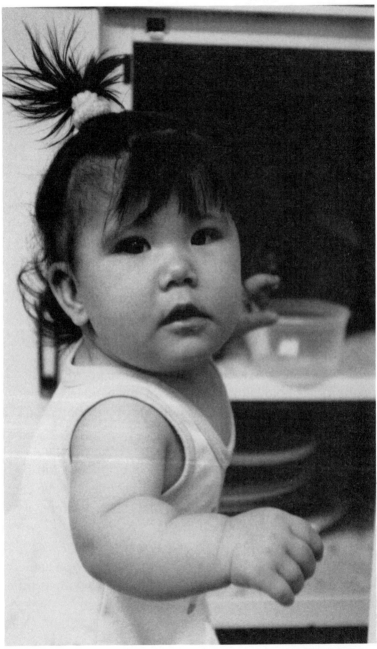

Making your home as accident-proof as possible is part of parenting.

Accident-Proofing Your Home

Accident-proofing your home is absolutely essential if you have a baby, toddler, or preschooler living there. Accidents injure and kill many young children every year. In fact, accidents are by far the greatest cause of injury and death for this age group—thousands are permanently crippled or killed annually.

The chief causes of fatal accidents for children under one year are suffocating and choking. Cars, fires, drowning, and poisoning cause the most fatal accidents for toddlers and preschoolers. Falls cause about 40 percent of all injuries.

Warning

Never leave baby alone on a changing table, bed, or other off-the-floor surface for a second. The baby who couldn't turn over yesterday may be able to do so today.

When you visit friends, put your tiny baby's blanket on the floor. She can nap there as well as she could on the bed, and she'll be much safer. She can't fall off the floor. Be sure she's protected from house pets and small children.

Your baby should not have a pillow in her bed. A pillow could cause a breathing problem if she got her face buried in it. If grandma made a beautifully embroidered pillow for her, appreciate it, but keep it out of her crib.

A propped bottle is dangerous for infants. Baby could choke from her milk coming too fast from that propped bottle. She could also choke on milk curds if she should spit up. She might be unable to clear her throat.

Start with the Kitchen

Dangers multiply rapidly when your child is crawling, then walking. Accident-proofing involves far more now that he can plunge so quickly into risky situations.

The kitchen is a marvelous learning laboratory for babies and toddlers. Designing it so it's safe for your baby is an important challenge. Hazards in many kitchens include:

- Cleaning supplies (Don't keep them in the cupboard under your sink.)
- Knives
- Vegetable grater
- Ice pick
- Cooking fork
- Hot pans (Keep the handles turned toward the back of the stove.)
- Coffee pot, toaster, and other appliance cords
- Iron and ironing board (Iron when baby is asleep, then put board and iron away.)
- Gas stove with controls baby can reach

Warning

If baby gets dishwashing detergent on his fingers, he'll put them in his mouth as usual. Because dishwashing detergent is so powerful, it can burn his mouth badly. Don't let it happen!

I keep a lock on the door under the sink so Gary can't get into it.

Jan, 15 - Gary, 12 months

My mother always said not to put my soaps and things in a low cupboard, so I have always kept them up high above the stove.

Olivia, 20 - Henry, 23 months

During the years you have a baby or young child, it is terribly important that you put such dangerous items in a high cupboard. Even there, if he's a climber, you should use a secure lock.

Leon pushes a chair up to the counter and gets up in the top cupboard looking for little goodies. I have glasses up there, so I suppose I'll have to fasten the doors shut. I keep him locked out of the bathroom.

Tamera, 21 - Leon, 20 months, and DeeDee, 41/2 years

When your child has a minor accident such as touching the stove and burning his fingers slightly, help him understand what happened. Don't say anything about "the bad stove" burning him, and don't fix it up with cookies. Sympathize, of course, but also explain that if he touches the stove when it's hot, he'll be burned.

Gas Stove Is Risky

If you're buying a range, you may be able to get one with controls on top at the back. If the controls are in

baby's reach, you'll have to watch constantly that he
doesn't turn the burner on. A gas stove without a self-
lighting device is extremely dangerous in a home with little
children. If it's turned on, but not lit, unburned gas will
escape into the room. This could cause an explosion or
asphyxiate people (cause them to stop breathing).

If you have a gas heater, have someone help you check
to see if it has a safety valve that shuts off the gas if the
pilot light goes out. If it doesn't have one and the pilot goes
out, the escaping unburned gas is toxic and can cause an
explosion.

The baby should not be left in a room with an unvented
gas heater because the gas (burned or unburned) will stay in
the room rather than going up a chimney or stack. Call your
gas company if you don't know whether your heater is
vented. For the same reason, you should not heat a room by
leaving a gas oven door open.

If you ever smell gas in your home, check with the gas
company immediately. In most areas, they will send
someone out to check it at no charge to you.

Other Hazards

*Sonja pulls on the tablecloth. If it were my own
home, I wouldn't leave it on the table. People tell me
kids have to learn not to touch it. I think when they're
babies you can't do that.*

                                        Julie, 16 - Sonja, 7 months

To a creeping baby, tablecloths are to be pulled. If hot
foods, even empty dishes, come down with the cloth,
results can be disastrous. Even placemats can cause big
problems. Our second son, when he was eleven months old,
pulled on a placemat early one winter morning. Over came
the cup of freshly poured coffee. His burn required
emergency hospital treatment.

You know how baby loves to play peek-a-boo by pulling
a blanket over his face. He might do the same thing if he
found a thin plastic bag. If he did, he could suffocate within
minutes. The plastic would cling to his face and he
wouldn't be able to breathe.

Carefully keep all plastic of this kind away from your
baby. Cut up and discard such bags immediately after you
get them, especially those put on the clothes at the dry
cleaner's.

---

*Never leave a baby or toddler
alone in the bathroom.*

Even if you lock up all medicines, you may decide the
bathroom is one room your baby can't enter. If she can't
open doors herself, just keep the door shut at all times.
Make it as safe as possible inside, however, because you
know she will get in there occasionally.

During the time she is pulling herself to stand, be especially careful to keep the bathroom door closed. It's possible for a toddler to pull herself up by the edge of the
toilet, lose her balance, fall in, and drown.

The day will come when your toddler goes into the
bathroom herself. She may even lock the door behind her.
A lock-release on the outside of the bathroom door would
solve that problem. Keep the release key where you can
find it quickly.

Check All Areas for Danger

Stairs are an obvious danger to a creeping/crawling/
toddling child. Putting a gate at the top and one at the
bottom is a solution. Put the lower gate at the second or
third step up, not at the bottom. Baby will then have a
chance to practice climbing a few steps, then coming back

down. He won't have far enough to fall to hurt himself, especially if there's a soft rug at the bottom.

Another room you may decide to shut off, perhaps with a gate, is where an older brother or sister plays. Satisfying baby's curiosity there might cause more trouble with big sister than it's worth. If big sister is only a few years older, she can't be expected to understand completely what childproofing means. Besides, big sister should not be expected to share her things, particularly not without her permission.

It takes pretty constant watching where I'm living. Quentin (Heidi's uncle) leaves little screws and things on the floor in his bedroom. I've asked him a few times to pick them up, but he doesn't. I get furious and start yelling at him.

Jenny, 18 - Heidi, 13 months

If you have a fireplace, open heater, heating register, or floor furnace, put guards in front of and over it. Use furniture to block off radiators.

If your toddler has learned to open doors, you can attach fasteners, the hook-and-eye kind, up too high for him to reach. You'll need some method of keeping doors closed if they lead to stairways, driveways, and some storage areas. Your window and door screens should be securely fastened. If your house has bars on the windows, they need to be the kind that can be opened from the inside.

Do you have a pet door, a little door your dog or cat can open? If it's big enough for your baby to get through, expect him to use it!

Sometimes I'll be doing something, curling my hair or polishing my nails. The next thing I know, Heidi has gone out the doggy door and is playing with the dogs in the back yard. I'll bring her back, and she'll do it again.

Jenny

Accident-Proof Outside Areas

A fenced-in yard is a marvelous luxury for a toddler and her parents. If you're lucky enough to have one, enjoy it, but keep an eye on your child as she plays there.

Some plants, such as poinsettia, caster beans, and oleander, are poisonous.

Yards, fenced or not, and garages need to be child-proofed, too. Check for rubbish, insecticides, paint removers, and other poisons. Get rid of them or lock them up. Nails, screws, and other hardware, assorted car parts, tools, and gardening equipment should be stored out of reach or locked in the garage.

Also get rid of rusty or tippy furniture. Check hammocks, swings, and other play equipment regularly for safety.

Some plants are poisonous such as poinsettia, caster beans, and oleander. Does your yard have shrubbery or other plants dangerous to your child? Also check any house plants in your home.

Even a lovely rose garden can harm a toddler when she runs into all those thorns. Putting a temporary, but sturdy fence around your roses will protect baby. It will also protect the roses.

Is Paint Lead-Free?

Do you have furniture, walls, or woodwork in your home which were painted before 1970? If the paint contains lead, it can damage your child if he chews on the painted surface, or if the paint is peeling and he puts bits of it in his mouth. Lead poisoning can be the result, a serious problem for babies and children.

Even though more recent coats of paint in old houses are probably lead-free, chipping paint can include the bottom

layers of lead-base paint. Many children eat these chips of
peeling paint and plaster. Apparently they taste sweet, and
children like them.

Glazed ceramic dishes imported from other countries
may have lead in the glaze, lead which may contaminate
food cooked or served in the dish.

If children get too much lead, they show signs of lead
poisoning. "Too much" for a baby may be a very little bit
of the paint. The child may become anemic and lose his
appetite. He may be either listless or hyperactive and irrit-
able. He may find it harder to learn, and may suffer convul-
sions and permanent brain damage from the poisoning.

If you suspect lead poisoning, check with your doctor.
Through a simple blood test, s/he can detect the condition.
If lead poisoning
has occurred, the
doctor can recom-
mend treatment to
get rid of much of
the extra lead in
your child's body
so he won't have
the problems
described above.

Car Safety

Of course
you'll do every-
thing you can to
keep your toddler
from running out
into the street. But
did you know that

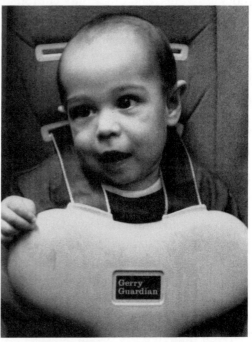

He's buckled in and ready for a ride.

more children are hurt inside cars as passengers than are injured on the outside as pedestrians?

Traffic accidents are the leading cause of death in childhood once the critical early months have passed. They claim more lives than any disease. In addition, hundreds of thousands are injured. Many remain permanently disabled, physically and/or mentally.

You can protect your child from injury while riding in your car by putting him in a safety-approved car seat (*not* a car bed).

For infants, you need a seat in which the baby rides facing backward in a semi-reclining position. It should be held firmly in place by the car's seat belt. When you choose a car seat for toddlers and slightly older children, too, be sure the seat can be fastened securely by the car's seat belt. In most states, babies and toddlers are required by law to be fastened in a car seat when riding in a car.

A car seat, of course, is safe only if the child is buckled in it. When your toddler decides to be negative about his car seat, it's time for you to be positive. Fasten him in it matter-of-factly, even if he's screaming. Be sure he knows you, too, use a seat belt.

Safety—A Big Responsibility

Making sure your child is safe in your home, in your car, everywhere he goes, is a big responsibility. Creating a safe environment that also allows him to explore and to learn about his world is a double challenge with double rewards.

You will find more peace of mind knowing your child is not in danger, and you will be delighted with the bright, happy individual that he is.

Her first steps—and soon she'll be running.

He's Into Everything!

Gary has been walking since he was ten months old. He says "Ma-ma," "Pa-pa." We talk to him a lot in both English and Spanish. He's curious. If he sees you doing something, he copies you. He'll come over and look. He's very close to me.

He climbs up on a board and then jumps off, but he's not on the couches yet. He loves playing outside with other kids. He takes pans out of the cupboard and takes them outside. He picks up a lot of rocks and puts them in the pans and carries them around.

Jan, 15 - Gary, 12 months

Robin's a monster. She gets into everything. She's crawling around, pulling herself up, standing up, grabbing all sorts of things.

Melinda, 16 - Robin, 9 months

This is the busiest stage yet for both you and your child.
She no longer is an infant. She's finally able to move—and
move she will. In just a few months, in fact, she may
be running.

Difficult Stage for Parents

This is a difficult stage for many parents. "She gets into
everything," they say. Because she can get into so many
things, people assume she should be able to understand
wrong from right. She should be able to follow your orders.

This isn't true. Her memory is only beginning to develop. If she does happen to remember that you said "No"
the last time she touched that ash tray, she still doesn't have
the self-control to leave such an inviting item alone. Slap-
ping her hand mostly teaches her that big people hit little
people. She really doesn't know why.

At this point, removing her from temptation is the smart
and loving approach. You can offer her a safe toy or activity instead of the forbidden one. Chances are pretty good
that she'll accept the change.

He Learns by Satisfying His Curiosity

Every parent has a huge responsibility to make it possible for her/his child to be as curious as possible. Curiosity
doesn't thrive on a steady diet of "No" or constant
imprisonment in a playpen.

Dale is curious about everything. He never stops,
doesn't want anyone to pick him up. He's independent
already. He has to see what everything feels like,
what it looks like. He gets Cheerios, and loves to play
with them.

He pulls the drawers open and takes clothes out.
He's trying to drink out of a cup, too.

Arlene, 17 - Dale, 11 months

Why is he so curious? Why does he have such a tremendous need to explore? Perhaps because he spent several months lying down, then sitting, but unable to move about. As he watched his world, he became more and more curious. Now that he's crawling, he can do something about his curiosity—he can explore. And explore he will.

You'll be amazed at the extent of his curiosity. He may turn the television on and off over and over again until you can stand it no longer. Think of the power he must feel when he pushes that button and the TV comes on!

He may open and shut a kitchen cupboard door dozens of times a day. If he finds paper on the floor, he'll crumple it. He'll investigate anything and everything.

Danette likes the wastebasket. She knocks it over and pounds on it. She opens the cupboard doors over and over and looks in. She'll stare, then grab something and walk away with it.

Caroline, 18 - Danette, 10 months

Robin swings doors back and forth. She smacks the bathroom door against the bathtub every morning and wakes my brother up. She'll do that for as long as she gets away with it.

Melinda

You'll probably see your baby staring intently at tiny particles. As she crawls across the floor, she'll pick up that speck of dust or the crumb she dropped from her high chair earlier. During this period, you may find yourself keeping your floors cleaner than you ever dreamed possible.

Jay picks up fuzz balls off the floor, string, that one little thing is what catches his eye. He loves newspapers, loves tearing them up.

Bev, 17 - Jay, 8 months

Into-Everything Stage

By the end of the first year, baby may be climbing. At first he will struggle to get on a low footstool. Soon he will master heights of a foot or so. If he can do that, he can climb on a chair. From there, he can climb to the table or to the kitchen counter. If you haven't baby-proofed your house and your habits, you now have a problem.

> *Dale climbs up on the bed and on the couch, and he's trying to get on the table. I worry about him because he won't stay still at all, and I'm afraid he'll get into something. I watch him constantly.*
>
> Arlene

> *I worry about Robin all the time. She gets into everything, and she's on the go 24 hours a day. She falls and gets hurt because she tries to stand up on everything. She climbs on the couch. She climbs up*

Her home is child-proofed—she can explore to her heart's content.

me when I'm holding her in the rocking chair—she
wants to climb up and look over the back.

Melinda

Has he learned to climb stairs? Then it's time to teach
him to come down safely. Show him how to slide down on
his stomach, feet first. Even if you have a gate on the stairs,
it may be left open occasionally, and he needs to learn.

Alice learned how to crawl up and down stairs
while we were in Texas, and she did it over and over.
At first, it scared me. She went up three stairs, and I
panicked and took her down. Then she started up
again and fell once. From then on, she could do it.

Melanie, 15 - Alice, 13 months

A one-year-old child is constantly active and constantly
moving. He's always completely absorbed in what he's
doing. He can be a fun companion because he is so active.
He can also be completely frustrating to you for the same
reason—he's so active.

Changing baby's diaper is quite a challenge during this
stage. Putting a toy in his hand may distract him from his
violent kicking and wriggling. You may even find you can
put a diaper on baby while he's standing up.

If all of this sounds as though baby is always in com-
mand, don't you believe it! Discipline is so important from
infancy on that *Teens Parenting—Discipline from Birth to
Three* is devoted entirely to this subject.

Of course he'll try to do some things that must be
stopped with a "No." However, his understanding of "No,"
if he hears it constantly, may be "Don't try" or "Don't
find out."

He won't learn as he should if he decides he isn't supposed to explore, to try new things. But he can certainly
cope with the truly necessary "No."

Cruising and Walking

*Alice isn't walking yet, but she takes a couple of
steps. She holds on to the couch and reaches, then
goes from the couch to the table. She's been doing
this since she was about nine months old.*

Melanie

Soon after baby learns to stand, she may start cruising.
To cruise, she walks around while carefully supporting
herself by placing her hands on the couch, a chair, or some
other object. A few babies go from crawling directly to
walking. But most cruise, sometimes for several weeks,
even months. At first she's extremely cautious, but before
long she skims along hand-over-hand the entire length of
the couch.

She'd love to have you arrange your living room furniture so she can cruise all around the room. Set the furniture
close enough together to allow her to reach from one to
the other.

*Danette is walking. At about eight months, she
started walking around or to the furniture. She took
her first steps three or four weeks later. For a couple
of weeks, she just took a few steps; then she started
walking all over the place.*

Caroline

Walking at nine months is unusual. The average age to
start walking is between twelve and fourteen months. Some
children wait a couple of months longer.

Constant Supervision Needed

Your toddler requires even more constant supervision
than she did when she was crawling. She will run outside to
explore. By herself, she would run into a busy street. What
can you do about this? *Supervise her!*

Try to be tolerant. Remember how curious she is and how impossible it is for her to control her own actions at this age. Baby's increased activities are often a worry:

I worry about Maelynn getting hurt, but I try not to be overprotective. I worry about her falling down, but when she falls, I say, "Oh, oh, you fell." I don't make a big scene out of it.

I have an aunt who says, "Oh, did you get hurt? Oh no!" and this scares her kids more. I try to stay real calm so Maelynn won't get scared. I've watched my cousins—after they fall, they keep playing until their mother screams, then they start crying. I'm learning a lot from them, and I don't want Maelynn to be like them.

Joleen, 17 - Maelynn, 9 months

He loves to play in the water.

Your baby continues to like water play. Now that she's older, this can be a problem if there is a pool nearby. A child can drown in a couple of inches of water. Always be with her when she's playing in water, whether it's in a tiny pool or a big one, or even in a bathtub or a pail of water.

Keeping Baby Clean . . . Enough

Trying to keep an exploring toddler soap-and-water clean at all times can upset her. It may also turn her into a child who is afraid of getting dirty—which limits drastically the amount of exploring she can do.

Buy or make the toughest and simplest clothes possible for your little toddler. Make sure she doesn't feel guilty if she gets herself and her clothes dirty. This is *not* a stay-clean stage!

It's important, though, that you protect your child from an overdose of harmful bacteria (germs).

While there are bacteria everywhere, most of them are harmless. The body can cope with them. The body can also cope with a few "bad" bacteria. If these bad ones have a good breeding place, they multiply rapidly. That's dangerous for baby. Good breeding grounds are food and feces.

Cooked food must be kept covered and cold or hot, never warm. If a tiny bite of cream pie falls under the table and you miss it when you clean, bacteria will start multiplying. If baby picks that tiny piece of pie up several hours later and stuffs it in her mouth, it may make her very sick.

Be extra careful about cleanliness in the bathroom, too. Be sure you always wash your hands after you change her diaper. Wash her hands for her if she explores her own body while you change her. Mop up toilet accidents and burped-up milk quickly.

Always clean up pet feces immediately. This may mean inspecting your yard every morning, even several times a day, if your toddler plays there. Children can get pin worms from handling pet feces.

Stranger Anxiety

He still loves people—for awhile. But by about eight months of age, your friendly baby may suddenly refuse to look at strangers. Perhaps he won't even go to grandma. Has he turned into a frightened, timid child?

Not really. But he has matured enough to know exactly whom he trusts. He generally trusts the people he lives with and who take care of him most of the time. Now he doubts the others. Sometimes this is labeled "stranger anxiety."

Maelynn likes to play with people she knows, but she's afraid of other people. She'll smile at them, but when they come up to get her, she'll hug me and not let them pick her up. You can see she's afraid, but she won't cry if she knows I'm there. I explain to her, and she seems to understand.

Joleen

Give baby time. If he hides his head in your shoulder as grandma holds out her arms to him, tell her he needs a few minutes to adjust. He'll go to her under his own terms.

Dependent on Mother

Toward the end of her first year, she may seem very dependent on mother. She can't bear to see you leave. She follows you all day long.

When you take her to visit a friend, she may spend the entire time in your arms. Only babies with good attachment to their mothers act this way. It's entirely normal, and if she needs you, she needs you.

I leave the room and Robin follows me because she's so nosy. She wants to know where I'm going.

*She'll follow me into the bathroom and stand and
beat on the tub. You say "No" to her, and she'll give
you a real dirty look, then cry.*

*If somebody does something she doesn't like, she
will crawl over to me and want me to pick her up. She
doesn't just cry, she screams.*

Melinda

This clinging-to-mother stage makes it hard to leave the
baby. It's not a good idea to leave while she's sleeping.
When she wakes up to find a babysitter instead of mother,
she may be very unhappy and frightened. It's far better to
hire the sitter to come to your home a half-hour before you
leave. Then baby has a better chance to adjust to the
situation. If she does cry as you leave, your sitter may
report that she started playing happily by the time your car
was out of sight.

Playing peek-a-boo with baby from early infancy may
help her realize that if you go away, you come back.   It
takes time to understand the important idea that, if they
leave, mother and dad really do come back.

Toilet Training? Not Yet!

Toilet training has not been mentioned in these chapters
because most children aren't ready to use the toilet by
themselves until they're past two years old. Some aren't
ready until they're three.

Trying to toilet train a child before s/he's ready will
most likely end in a lot of frustration for both of you.
Unsuccessful toilet training efforts, in fact, are probably
one of the biggest problems leading to child abuse.

Don't be in a hurry. Wait until your child lets you know
s/he is ready. See *Teens Parenting—Discipline from Birth
to Three* for an in-depth discussion of this subject.

Less Sleep Needed Now

Your child needs less sleep as he grows older. By his first birthday, he'll probably need only one nap per day. Some babies want to nap in the morning. Then they get fussy by mid-afternoon. If you put him down for a second nap, he's awake later and later in the evening.

If you would like to have him in bed at a "decent" hour at night, try keeping him awake a little longer in the morning. Then feed him a light lunch, perhaps at 10:30 a.m., before his nap. When he wakes two hours or so later, give him another light lunch. He may last until early supper, then go to bed for the night.

The morning nap can gradually be pushed to a later time. Before long, he may be able to wait until noon for lunch, then have his nap. This is important to a lot of parents. Much as they love him, they like having their evenings free of the constant child care they experience all day long.

Danette used to go to bed at 7:00, but lately she's started going at 8:00. I give her supper. She plays for quite awhile, then at 8 o'clock I give her a bottle. After she drinks her milk, she kisses me good night, and I put her to bed.

She's very very good about sleeping. She'll go to bed at 8:00, wake up next morning at 6:30. She has a bottle, then plays until 8:00 or 8:30. Then she wants her breakfast.

A couple of months ago she started fussing at bedtime. I wanted her to go to bed at a certain time, so I would put her in her crib. She would cry, but I would leave her in her crib for perhaps ten minutes. That seemed like a long time, but she would get tired and go to sleep. After two or three nights, she started going to sleep right away.

Caroline

Bedtime Routine Is Important

Many active toddlers are *not* "very very good about sleeping." Probably at least half put up some fuss about going to bed, especially if other family members are still up.

It may take half an hour for her to unwind, to relax enough to go to sleep.

Many parents prefer to have their small children in bed two or three hours before they go to sleep themselves. Most often a time between 6 p.m. and 8 p.m. is chosen. However,

a different schedule may work better for some parents.

Most important is that the child have a regular bedtime. You can't keep her up until 10:00 tonight, then expect her to lie down and go to sleep at 8 o'clock tomorrow night.

Following the same routine every night helps most children accept bedtime. Unless bathtime

A bedtime routine helps her get to sleep.

is a boisterous play session, bathing her before she goes to bed may relax her.

Does your baby have a favorite blanket or stuffed animal? Encourage her to take one special thing to bed with her. Most babies have a security blanket or other object that is important to them. Perhaps it's a loved teddy bear.

Attachment to the security object may begin in this eight-to-twelve month stage, although it will become much stronger later. Many mothers report that it's almost impossible to get that special blanket away from the child long enough to put it through the washing machine.

Help her find the blanket or teddy bear that is part of the going-to-bed ritual. Read her a story. Then feed her that last bottle of milk as you rock and sing or croon to her. It may take half an hour for her to unwind, to relax enough to go to sleep.

If she insists on taking her bottle to bed, remember the problem caused by milk dripping on her teeth all night. The milk film can cause serious tooth decay. If she insists on a bottle, you insist on putting water in it, not milk.

If you follow the same routine with your child every night, you may find she goes to bed fairly happily most of the time. Your evenings will be more pleasant, too, if putting your child to bed is not a struggle.

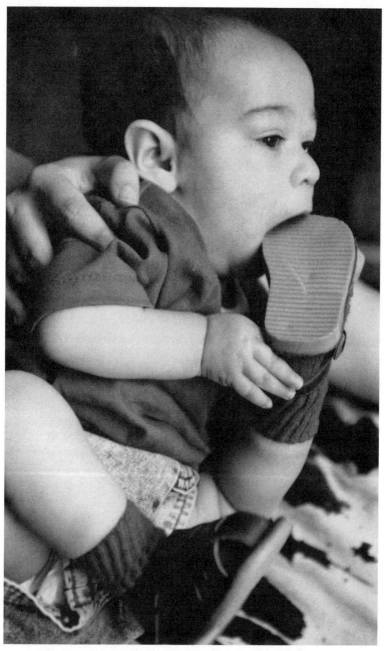

Mom and dad enjoy playing with him and teaching him.

Enjoying Your Child

I'm enjoying Danette more as the months go by—
she gets better and better! I go crazy with her new
toys. We sit on the rug and play all kinds of games. I
bounce her up and down on the bed.

Danette likes music. She likes to sing. I hold her
and dance with her a lot. I'm crazy with her.

We go outside and I chase her all over. Jim and I
hold her hands and run with her.

Caroline, 18 - Danette, 10 months

Outdoor Play

Most children this age love to play outdoors. If you don't
have a grassy yard, is there a park nearby? Of course, being
outside when you're one year old means lots of supervision
from mother, dad, or another caregiver.

*Dale loves being outside, and he likes the park a
lot. We go every Sunday because his father plays
baseball. We're constantly chasing after him.*

                                        Arlene, 17 - Dale, 11 months

Playing Together

She'll love playing with you. Because she likes to
imitate, she may enjoy playing follow-the-leader. Keep it
simple at first. Clap your hands, put a hat on your head, and
wave your arms.

Sounds interest your toddler, just as they have since she
was an infant. Wind chimes outside her bedroom window
are pleasant for her. Records, radio, music boxes, and bells
will intrigue her. "Singing" with you is great fun.

Dance with baby. Before she's standing or walking,
she'll love dancing in your arms. Later she'll entertain you
by dancing by herself.

Let her make her own "music" with a drum made from
an empty oatmeal box. Tape the lid on the box, then give
her a wooden spoon to use as a drum stick. Show her how
to play her drum.

Early in this stage, baby will love to pull a toy on a
string. When she's crawling, sometimes she'll go backward
so she can watch the toy as she pulls the string. If the toy
makes a noise as she pulls it, so much the better.

A favorite activity is emptying things. Your toddler will
empty dresser drawers, kitchen cupboards, bookshelves,
trash cans, whatever she can reach. As soon as you put
things back, she'll be ready to take them out again.

*I try to keep Dale out of cupboards. I put rubber
bands on them. He pulls the drawers right out and
takes clothes out. I tell him "No" and set him down,
but he goes right back and does it again.*

                                                            Arlene

Giving her a dresser drawer, a kitchen cupboard, and a bookshelf that are "hers" may help. Don't expect her to be satisfied only with emptying her toys, however. She'll like that kitchen cupboard a lot more if she can empty it of your pans and plastic containers. Of course you'll be sure all cleaning materials have been safely put away.

It may also help to give her a variety of containers to empty. Perhaps her toys can be kept in small boxes or baskets. Giving her many opportunities to empty things "legally" should help her learn not to empty and re-empty everything else in the house.

I'll fill a can or a box with a bunch of stuff. She likes to take one thing out at a time, play with it for awhile, then take something else out and play with it.

Caroline

Choosing Toys

One-year-olds like giant snap-lock rings and beads. They're also ready for big wooden or plastic blocks. They play with them mostly by putting them in and dumping them out of containers. Your toddler may be able to balance one block on top of another soon.

Balls are still the best toys for your child. Get him several in a variety of sizes from small ones (but too big to be swallowed) to big beach balls. He will love a simple game of catch with you.

Felt toys aren't good because the dye in the fabric usually isn't colorfast. Check your child's stuffed toys to be sure the eyes and ears are firmly attached. Does the animal have a bell around its neck or even a ribbon on which baby could choke? You need to take off any part of that toy that he could pull off.

A round cereal box makes a fine tunnel. Take the bottom off, then show baby how to push a car through his tunnel.

He'll watch for his car at the other end. Or you can tie a string to the car, put the string through the tunnel, and let him pull the car through.

You can also make a cardboard hill for his car. Fold the cardboard to set at a slant on the floor. Then show baby how to put the car at the top of the hill and let it roll down.

Time for Fingerpainting

Let him fingerpaint. He may be ready by the time he's a year old. Of course he'll taste and examine the paint first. Then he may paint a little.

Recipe

You can make a safe (from a tasting standpoint—it still makes a mess!) fingerpaint by mixing two tablespoons of cornstarch into two tablespoons of cold water. Then add one cup boiling water and stir again.

For color, use food coloring or powdered fruit drink. One tablespoon of yellow prepared mustard to two tablespoons of the base makes a canary yellow paint.

Finger painting takes some preparation. Put old clothes on your child and lots of newspapers on the floor. A small chair and table with lots of working space would be ideal, but a high chair will do.

Almost any kind of plain paper is all right for finger painting—brown wrapping paper, paper bags, cardboard from shirt and panty hose packages. Tape the paper down to the table or tray before baby starts painting.

After all this preparation, he may do more tasting than painting. You can show him how to use the paint on the paper. He may find the whole thing a bit weird, but he'll probably have a ball. He'll enjoy his fingerpainting even more if you paint with him.

Let Him Help

Trying to copy what you do is important to a toddler. At eight months, he explores everything for the joy of exploring. Almost everything is new to him. A few months later, he wants to follow adults' examples. Earlier he banged with a spoon; now he will stir with it like mom does.

Baby loves to do what you do. Let him "help" you as much as possible as you do your work. While you're cooking, set him in his high chair near you. Are you baking a pie or making tortillas? Give him a little piece of dough so he can work along with you. If you're stirring something, give him a small pan and a spoon so he, too, can stir.

Interacting with Others

Robin is really lovable. She gives kisses and hugs—and she spits at you if she really likes you!

Melinda, 15 - Robin, 9 months

Let her "help" you as much as possible as you work.

Busy as she is, your toddler will often show her affection for you and for others.

Toward the end of her first year, she probably will like being around other children. She may play by herself, but she'll enjoy watching the others. Sometimes she may try to join their fun.

Don't expect a toddler to share her toys with another child for a long time yet. She's still too busy learning about herself and her world to be able to understand why Johnnie, just because he's a guest, should play with her ball.

Do you have an older child? If he's more than three years older than the baby, he probably spends most of the time playing with children his age. When he does interact with the baby, he's probably quite gentle usually, and treats the baby like the baby she is.

A brother or sister not yet three, however, may show resentment and dislike for the baby. This stage is particularly difficult because the baby will constantly get into her brother's or sister's toys. She'll generally be a nuisance to your older toddler. The closer together the children are in age, the more hostile your older child may be.

As you supervise the two, remember that the older child, if he's under three, needs you almost as much as does the little one. You'll wonder at times how you can stretch your caring and your attention far enough for both.

Fusses between two toddlers are normal. A one-year-old and a two-year-old can't be expected to get along beautifully all the time, or even much of the time.

More Language Development

Dale gets into everything. He's starting to talk, to say words. The other night I said "Good night," and he said "Night!" That's exciting.

Arlene

If you have talked to baby ever since he was born, and you've given him lots of learning experiences, he'll be working hard learning to talk by the end of his first year. He won't be saying many words yet, but he'll try.

Researchers studied a group of mothers who read to their babies 15 to 20 minutes each day. They read from simple, inexpensive children's books, pointed at the pictures, and talked about them. They used the books as the basis for talking with their infants.

Language development of these children was compared with a carefully matched group of children who weren't in the study and whose mothers did not read to them consistently. By the time they were 17 months old, the children whose mothers had read to them had better speaking abilities than did the other group of children.

I read to Danette, especially Dr. Suess. I think reading to her gives her a head start in her education.

I enjoy sitting and reading with her. I read mostly at night, but a lot of times in the afternoon, too, we'll read a book. Often I sit in my rocking chair, she sits on my lap, and we read.

Caroline

Your Exciting Challenge

Loving, caring for, and guiding your child throughout her early life is an exciting challenge. Your baby has become a "real" person, a child who is on her way to becoming a self-sufficient individual. You are an important part of her growth as you love her, care for her, and enjoy games and activities with her.

Mom has a wonderful incentive for working toward her goals.

Working Toward Your Future

*It's harder being a single parent although Alice's
father has been helping me. But he's too serious—he
says within a year we should have this and that, and
we'll get married. But I'm not going to marry nobody.*

*This is what I want to do. I'm going to finish high
school in two years, I hope. Then I want to go to
nursing school. I don't want to be on welfare all my
life. I feel I want to make my own money.*

Melanie, 15 - Alice, 13 months

A mother who has her first child before she is 18 is
likely to be poor during much of her life. Many young
mothers find they must rely on welfare or minimum wage
for survival. In fact, in about half the families receiving
AFDC (Aid to Families with Dependent Children), the
mother had her first baby when she was a teenager.

However, it doesn't seem to be the early parenting that causes the poverty. *It's the lack of a good education and job skills.* That lack, of course, often goes hand in hand with early motherhood—and fatherhood.

Most young mothers of 15, or even 17, find it difficult to continue their education. An obvious reason is the lack of good child care in many areas. Even if a grandmother is available for babysitting during the day, a teenage mother will find high school life different and usually harder than it is for her non-parenting friends.

Often it's too difficult. A majority of the women in this country who deliver a child before age 18 never finish their high school education.

Continuing School Is Crucial

Statistics show that if a young mother completes her education and doesn't have additional children right away, she may do as well as her friends who delay childbearing until later. If she becomes pregnant at an early age, gets married, drops out of school, and has more children rather quickly, she's likely to have money problems throughout her life.

These are factors you may be able to control. You start with your own situation. If you are a young parent with a child to support and care for, that's where you start with your life planning.

If you aren't already married, you may decide to postpone your wedding. You may make sure you don't get pregnant again before you think you're ready for another baby. And you can do everything possible to continue your education.

My future plans are to go back to school and get my high school diploma. I need to do this because it's a feeling I just can't shake off. It's like an itch that I

*can't scratch. In other words, I need to do it for my
peace of mind.*

Deborah, 16 - 7 months pregnant

*I want to finish school for sure. It will be hard, but
I've got to finish. I want some kind of secretarial job,
but I'll stay home with the baby for awhile. At first I
want a part-time job. Then when Racquelle starts
school, I'll work full-time.*

Cheryl, 15 - Racquelle, 2 months

Marriage May Limit Schooling

High school mothers who get married are far more likely
to drop out of school than are their single friends. Of those
who are neither wives nor mothers, less than 10 percent
drop out before finishing high school.

A higher percentage of unmarried teenagers who have a
baby never graduate from high school. And even more of
those who marry—a whopping 80 percent—quit school
before they graduate.

Nearly half of all families headed by women live in
poverty. Women without a high school education are more
likely to head a family than are women who graduated. Yet
these women with less education won't be able to earn as
much as will their better-educated friends.

It seems ironic—if she doesn't have an education, she
can't earn as much money. Yet she is more likely to be the
sole wage earner for her family. Life isn't always fair.

Day Care Desperately Needed

Most young parents need day care services in order to
complete their high school education. Day care isn't available for teenage parents in most school districts in
the country.

---

*The lack of day-care services condemns
many young parents to reliance
on welfare income for survival.*

Finding day care for her child is a serious problem for
many young mothers. They need to continue their education, acquire job skills, and work in order to be self-
supporting. To do this, they must have day care for their
children. The lack of day-care services condemns many
young parents to reliance on welfare income for survival.

Some young parents have a mother who is home at least
part of the time. Alison's mother works, but is home by
early afternoon. She is willing to take care of Stevie when
she gets home, so Alison has planned a work schedule
which will permit her to be home with her son during much
of his waking time:

> *I'm going to look for a job soon as a hospital ward
> clerk. I'll try to get swing shift so I can be here most
> of the day with Stevie. My mother comes home from
> work by mid-afternoon. She could take care of Stevie
> when I go to work.*
>
> *He stays up late, so I could put him to bed when
> I get home at 10 or 11 p.m. I'd like to be able to
> do that.*

Alison, 18 - Stevie, 2 months

If Relatives Can't Help

Many grandparents, of course, are not available for
babysitting. In the first place, they may not want to care for
a child. Perhaps your mother feels she has raised her family
and she doesn't want to start over again. You can probably
understand her feelings.

Some schools have infant care on campus.

Even if she's willing to babysit, grandma may have a job herself. Everyone in your family may already be working. There may be no one at home who will/can take care of your baby for you.

Unless you're one of the lucky few teenage parents in this country whose school offers child care for its students' babies, you have a real problem. You know how important it is to continue your education. Perhaps you've finished high school, but you want to get further job training or go on to college. You may be ready to get a job now, and you don't want to settle for staying home and living on welfare income.

Who will care for your child while you're in school or working?

Most day care centers are for children who are at least two years old. Many will only accept children who are toilet trained. Your community may not even have a child-care center which takes babies and toddlers. To find out, check with your school district and family service agencies.

Family day care may be available. In this arrangement, a person cares for a small number of children in her/his own home. Some day care homes are licensed, some are not.

In order to provide good day care, one person should be responsible for no more than five children including her/his own. No more than two of these children should be under two years of age.

If you can afford it, you might prefer to find a caregiver who will come to your home to care for your child. Babies and toddlers aren't likely to want the same schedule as you must follow. Being able to let your child sleep while you go on to school could be good for both of you.

Choosing a Caregiver

The decision you make about day care for your child is extremely important. Yet some people appear to put less thought into selecting a caregiver for their child than they do in buying a car! Whether you choose a day care center, family day care, or a caregiver who comes to your home, be sure you put a lot of thought into your choice.

Ask questions, lots of them. Don't hire the first person you find. Talk to several caregivers, then choose the one you think would be best for your child. One mother described her search for a caregiver for her small son:

I started answering other people's ads in our local paper. Then I ran an ad myself, and that was how I met the best ones.

When people called me, I would ask them a bunch of questions. I could tell from that first telephone conversation that I didn't want some of them. I interviewed at least twenty people before I decided.

I had lots of questions:

  • *How many kids do you care for?*

- *How old are they?*
- *How do you discipline children?*
- *What do you do when a baby cries?*
- *When my son starts crawling, how will you protect your house? (If she said she used a playpen, I usually marked her off my list.)*

If I liked what she said on the phone, I would visit her, preferably without a lot of advance notice. I wanted to see what her house was like, how she coped. If she cared for other kids, I would try to visit while they were there. If her house was too neat, I'd worry.

Of course I wanted to be sure she had a place for Bryan to eat, to sleep, to play. What kinds of activities would she have for toddlers? I asked all sorts of questions.

Tricia, 18 - Bryan, 6 months

Remember, you're the employer when you hire a caregiver. You're the one making the decision. You have the right to ask about anything that might have something to do with your child's welfare. Ideally, you'll be able to find someone who will care for and love your child in much the same way as you do when you're with him.

Even if he's older, you need to know as much as possible about his "other home."

Before you make your selection, be sure to ask if the caregiver takes care of sick children. If she doesn't, perhaps you have a friend or someone in your family who is willing to be on call for babysitting during minor illnesses. Babies and children get sick at inconvenient times.

Once you find a caregiver, will you continue checking on the kind of care your child is receiving? If he isn't talking yet, he can't tell you what is going on when you're gone. Even if he's older, you need to know as much as possible about his "other home."

You could make excuses to visit your child occasionally at unexpected times. This is one way to learn about the kind of care he's receiving. A good caregiver should welcome your interest and concern.

Paying for Child Care

Finding child care is one thing. Paying for it is another. If you qualify for AFDC, talk to your social worker. There may be extra money available for child care while you continue your education or learn job skills.

Her school district provides child care and transportation.

If you're on welfare, perhaps you could get into a program that provides assistance with on-the-job training. Such a program might provide extra help with child care, transportation, and other job related expenses while you're in school or in job training.

If you can't afford to pay a caregiver, and you have no one who will take care of your child at no charge, can you trade child care duties with another young parent? It would be hard to make such an arrangement work if you need to attend high school full-time. If you're interested in attending night school, or if you're a college student, a trade might work.

Schedule your classes so you can care for the other child while her mother is in class. Then she can be responsible for yours while you go to school. Caring for two children while you're trying to study would be difficult. It could be a way, however, to get that education you need so badly for your child's sake as well as your own.

Planning Your Family

I'm going to have two children at the most. I think two is enough. I think ideally I would have another one when Dale's about three—when he more or less does things on his own.

Arlene, 17 - Dale, 11 months

Many teen mothers and fathers who have one child are able to continue their education and work toward their goals. If they have a second child before they have finished school, the difficulties multiply. Having more than one child limits one's independence drastically:

It's really hard—a second kid seems like five more. I guess I shouldn't have had her. I tell Charles, "You were right—I should have had an abortion."

*I wanted to get everything over with—graduate, get
my license, have the two kids. But now I don't really
have anything. I'm tired and nervous and crabby.*
                        Colleen 18 - Ruby, 7 months; Hilda, 21 months

The money cost of having a second baby soon after the
first can be overwhelming:

*You don't think the expense of a second baby is
that much, but it is. It costs a lot more with Ruby.
Charles used to work overtime last year for extras
like Christmas. Now he has to work overtime so we
can make it through the month.*

*Maybe it wouldn't be so bad if we were living in a
house and had a lot of things, then said, "We're
broke." But it shouldn't happen when we're in a one-
bedroom apartment. You wouldn't believe what it
costs for these two kids.*
                                                      Colleen

From baby's standpoint, waiting three or even four years
before the next child is wise. A two-year-old needs about as
much care—in different ways—as does an infant.

*When we brought Leon home from the hospital,
DeeDee was almost three. She wanted to hold him, so
we set her down on the couch and propped a pillow
on her so she could. Ever since, he's been her baby.
We've had very little jealousy.*

*If we had had him sooner, DeeDee couldn't have
enjoyed being a baby long enough. I wanted her to be
a little more independent so she would be used to my
not spending so much time with her.*

*A lot of mothers I've seen have their kids real close
together. It kind of makes the oldest child feel ne-
glected. The little baby has to grow up so fast instead
of enjoying being a baby.*
                        Tamera, 21 - Leon, 20 months; DeeDee, 4 years

Babies do come by accident. If you don't want another child right away, birth control is essential. This could be simply not having intercourse, but most parents will want some other kind of contraceptive. If you're breastfeeding, don't count on it to keep you from getting pregnant. You can get pregnant even though you're breastfeeding.

If you're breastfeeding, check with your doctor about taking the birth control pill. Some pills are likely to cut down on your milk supply. A different dosage, however, might be all right for you while you breastfeed.

This might be a good time to ask your doctor about inserting an IUD (intrauterine device). Or you might consider the contraceptive implant. Check with your doctor.

If the man uses a condom (rubber) and the woman uses foam, the two methods together are as successful at preventing conception as is the pill or the I.U.D. Both the condom and foam can be bought at a drugstore with no prescription from the doctor.

For more information on birth control methods, see *Teens Parenting: Your Pregnancy and Newborn Journey.*

Sexually active couples need to discuss their thinking concerning contraception. If this is difficult for you, remember that having another baby too soon would also be hard on your partner. Brad talked about this issue:

I'd rather have three years between children. I want my first son to have time for me to teach him.

How to talk about sex? First of all, be alone. Ask him how he feels about using protection. How many kids do you want to have? If one or the other doesn't want to use protection, they have to talk it through.

Brad, 17 - Maria, 13 months (Carole, 16)

If you aren't pregnant now, and you don't want to have a child soon, you have two choices. One, of course, is not to have sex. If you're having sex, use birth control—*always.*

Your Long-Range Goals

Long-range goals are important too. Where do you want to be in five years? The problem with long-range goals, however, is that they're too easy. You might say, "In five years, I'll be out of school, married, and living in a big house. We'll have another baby. Doug will be working and I'll stay home with the children."

That's a long-range goal, and if this is what you want, by all means continue planning and working toward it.

Most important, what are you doing this year, *this month* to work toward the life you want for yourself and your child? What must you do in order to continue your education? What steps can you take *now* to begin or continue your job skills training?

If you and your baby's other parent are together, you both need to continue your education and job skills training—unless, of course, one or both of you is already job-ready.

Sometimes young mothers still think they won't have to get a job because their baby's father will support them. For most of us, this is not a realistic expectation for several reasons:

- Many two-parent families find both parents must work to support their family.

- The majority of teenage marriages end within a short time.

- As a parent, you need to be educated in order to be the best possible parent to your child.

What are you doing today to make a satisfying future for yourself and your child?

Appendix

About The Author

Jeanne Warren Lindsay, M.A., C.H.E., developed and for sixteen years coordinated the Teen Mother Program, an alternative offered to pregnant and parenting students in the ABC Unified School District, Cerritos, California. This program is a choice offered to pregnant and parenting students who do not wish to attend the comprehensive high school throughout pregnancy. Ms. Lindsay has counseled hundreds of pregnant teenagers and teenage parents, and she continues as an active consultant in the program.

Ms. Lindsay has advanced degrees in home economics and anthropology. She edited the *NOAPP Network,* quarterly newsletter of the National Organization on Adolescent Pregnancy and Parenting 1983-1990, and she currently edits *PPT Express,* a newsletter for teachers and others working with pregnant and parenting teens. She frequently gives presentations across the country on the culture of school-age parents, teenage marriage, educating pregnant and parenting teens, and other topics.

Ms. Lindsay is the author or co-author of thirteen other books on adolescent pregnancy and parenting, teenage marriage, and adoption from the birthfamily's perspective. Titles are listed on page 2.

Jeanne and Bob have been married for 40 years. They have five children and five gorgeous grandchildren.

Bibliography

Dozens of books on parenting are published each year. Following are a few which may be of special interest to teenage parents. If you can't find a book you want in your bookstore, you usually can order it directly from the publisher. Enclose $2 for shipping in addition to price of the book.

Brenner, Erma. *When Baby Comes Home: Your First Year as a Parent*. 1984. 128 pp. Janus Book Publishers, 2501 Industrial Parkway West, Hayward, CA 94545.

> Beautifully illustrated by Symeon Shimin. Simply written book for new parents.

Green, Martin I. *A Sigh of Relief: The First-Aid Handbook for Childhood Emergencies*. 1989. 264 pp. Bantam Books, 666 Fifth Avenue, New York, NY 10103.

> Lots of illustrations and information about all sorts of things. Easy to find suggestions for treating childhood emergencies.

Brinkley, Ginny, and Sherry Sampson. *You and Your New Baby: A Book for Young Mothers.* 1991. 80 pp. Pink Ink! P.O. Box 866, Atlantic Beach, FL 32233-0866.

Simple guide for caring for baby. Written for teen parents with an easy-to-understand format.

Lansky, Vickie. *Getting Your Child to Sleep . . . and Back to Sleep.* 1991. 132 pp. The Book Peddlers, 18326 Minnetonka Boulevard, Deephaven, MN 33391.

Many good suggestions for dealing with babies and small children who don't sleep much.

Leach, Penelope. *Your Baby and Child from Birth to Age Five.* Revised, 1989. 554 pp. Alfred A. Knopf.

An absolutely beautiful book packed with information, many color photos and lovely drawings. Comprehensive, authoritative, and outstandingly sensitive guide to child care and development.

Lindsay, Jeanne Warren. *Do I Have a Daddy? A Story About a Single-Parent Child.* 1991. 48 pp. Morning Glory Press, 6595 San Haroldo Way, Buena Park, CA 90620.

A beautiful book for the child who has never met his/her father. A special sixteen-page section offers suggestions to single mothers. Also available in Spanish: *¿Yo tengo papá?*

_____. *School-Age Parents: The Challenge of Three-Generation Living.* 1990. 224 pp. Morning Glory Press.

A much needed book for dealing with the frustrations, problems, and pleasures of three-generation living.

_____. *Teenage Couples—Coping with Reality: Dealing with Money, In-Laws, Babies and Other*

***Details of Daily Life. Teenage Couples—Caring,
Commitment and Change: How to Build a Rela-
tionship that Lasts.*** 1995. 192 pp. ea. Morning
Glory Press.

Relationship books written especially for teenagers. Based on
in-depth interviews with married teens and on nationwide
survey of nearly 4,000 teenagers' attitudes toward marriage.

_____. ***Teen Dads: Rights, Responsibilities and Joys.***
1993. 192 pp. Morning Glory Press.

A how-to-parent book from conception to age 3 of the child,
written especially for teenage fathers.

_____. ***Teens Parenting—The Challenge of Toddlers.***
1991. 192 pp. each. Morning Glory Press.

How to parent toddlers, written especially for teenage parents.

_____ and Jean Brunelli. ***Teens Parenting—Your
Pregnancy and Newborn Journey.*** 1994. Morning
Glory Press.

Prenatal health book for pregnant teenagers. Includes section
on care of the newborn and a chapter for fathers. Also available in Easier Reading and Spanish editions (***Adolescentes
como padres—La jornada de tu embarazo y el nacimiento de
tu bebé***).

_____ and Sally McCullough. ***Teens Parenting—
Discipline from Birth to Three.*** 1991. 192 pp.
Morning Glory Press.

Provides teenage parents with guidelines to help prevent
discipline problems with their children and guidelines for
dealing with problems when they occur.

MELD Parenting Materials. Nueva Familia: Six books in
Spanish and English. ***Baby Is Here. Feeding Your
Child, 5 months-2 years. Healthy Child, Sick***

Child. Safe Child and Emergencies. Baby Grows, Baby Plays. 1992. $9 each. MELD, 123 North Third Street, Suite 507, Minneapolis, MN 55401. 612/332-7563.

Very easy to read books full of information. Designed especially for Mexican and Mexican American families, but excellent for anyone with limited reading skills. Ask for catalog of other resources for school-age parents.

Reynolds, Marilyn. *Detour for Emmy.* 1993. 156 pp. Morning Glory Press.

Wonderful novel about a 15-year-old who has a baby and finds her life changes drastically.

_____. *Too Soon for Jeff.* 1994. 224 pp. Morning Glory Press.

Novel about a reluctant teenage father.

Parent Express Series. ANR Publications, University of California, 6701 San Pablo Avenue, Oakland, CA 94608-1239.

Wonderful series of newsletters for parents. The first set starts two months before delivery and continues through the first year of the child's life. Second set covers second and third years.

Renfrew, Mary, Chloe Fisher, Suzanne Arms. *Bestfeeding: Getting Breastfeeding Right for You.* 1990. 225 pp. Celestial Arts Publishing, P.O. Box 7327, Berkeley, CA 94707.

Good description, with lots of photographs and drawings, of the importance of breastfeeding and of how to make the process work.

For a more extended bibliography, see
You Can Help Pregnant and Parenting Teens, Book 2: Curriculum Guide for Teens Parenting Series.

Index

OTHER RESOURCES FROM MORNING GLORY PRESS

TEENAGE COUPLES—Caring, Commitment and Change: How to Build a Relationship that Lasts. TEENAGE COUPLES— Coping with Reality: Dealing with Money, In-Laws, Babies and Other Details of Daily Life.
Two books to help teenage couples develop healthy, loving and lasting relationships.

TEENS PARENTING—Your Pregnancy and Newborn Journey
How to take care of yourself and your newborn. For pregnant teens. Available in "regular" (RL 6), Easier Reading (RL 3), and Spanish.

TEENS PARENTING—Your Baby's First Year
TEENS PARENTING—The Challenge of Toddlers
TEENS PARENTING—Discipline from Birth to Three
Three how-to-parent books especially for teenage parents.

VIDEO: "Discipline from Birth to Three" supplements above book.

TEEN DADS: Rights, Responsibilities and Joys. Parenting book for teenage fathers.

DETOUR FOR EMMY. Novel about teenage pregnancy.

TOO SOON FOR JEFF. Novel from teen father's perspective.

SURVIVING TEEN PREGNANCY: Choices, Dreams, Decisions
For all pregnant teens—help with decisions, moving on toward goals.

SCHOOL-AGE PARENTS: The Challenge of Three-Generation Living. Help for families when teen daughter (or son) has a child.

BREAKING FREE FROM PARTNER ABUSE. Guidance for victims of domestic violence.

DID MY FIRST MOTHER LOVE ME? A Story for an Adopted Child. Birthmother shares her reasons for placing her child.

DO I HAVE A DADDY? A Story About a Single-Parent Child
Picture/story book especially for children with only one parent. Also available in Spanish, *¿Yo tengo papá?*

OPEN ADOPTION: A Caring Option
A fascinating and sensitive account of the new world of adoption.

PREGNANT TOO SOON: Adoption Is an Option. Written to pregnant teens who may be considering an adoption plan.

ADOPTION AWARENESS: A Guide for Teachers, Counselors, Nurses and Caring Others. How to talk about adoption when no one is interested.

TEEN PREGNANCY CHALLENGE, Book One: Strategies for Change; Book Two: Programs for Kids. Practical guidelines for developing adolescent pregnancy prevention and care programs.

MORNING GLORY PRESS

6595 San Haroldo Way, Buena Park, CA 90620
714/828-1998 — FAX 714/828-2049

Please send me the following: Price   Total

Teenage Couples: Caring, Commitment and Change
____   Paper, 0-930934-93-8   9.95 _____
____   Cloth, ISBN 0-930934-92-x   15.95 _____
Teenage Couples: Coping with Reality
____   Paper, ISBN 0-930934-86-5   9.95 _____
____   Cloth, ISBN 0-930934-87-3   15.95 _____
___ *Too Soon for Jeff*   Paper, ISBN 0-930934-91-1   8.95 _____
____   Cloth, ISBN 0-930934-90-3   15.95 _____
__ *Detour for Emmy*   Paper, ISBN 0-930934-76-8   8.95 _____
____   Cloth, ISBN 0-930934-75-x   15.95 _____
__*Teen Dads*   Paper, ISBN 0-930934-78-4   9.95 _____
____   Cloth, ISBN 0-930934-77-6   15.95 _____
__ *Do I Have a Daddy?*   Cloth, ISBN 0-930934-45-8   12.95 _____
___*Did My First Mother Love Me?* ISBN 0-930934-85-7   12.95 _____
___*Breaking Free from Partner Abuse* 0-930934-74-1 $7.95 _____
___*Surviving Teen Pregnancy* Paper, 0-930934-47-4 $9.95_____
School-Age Parents: Three-Generation Living
____   Paper, ISBN 0-930934-36-9   10.95 _____
Teens Parenting—Your Pregnancy and Newborn Journey
____   Paper, ISBN 0-930934-50-4   9.95 _____
____   Cloth, ISBN 0-930934-51-2   15.95 _____
Easier Reading Edition—Pregnancy and Newborn Journey
____   Paper, ISBN 0-930934-61-x   9.95 _____
____   Cloth, ISBN 0-930934-62-8   15.95 _____
Spanish—Adolescentes como padres—La jornada . . .
____   Paper, ISBN 0-930934-69-5   9.95 _____
Teens Parenting—Your Baby's First Year
____   Paper, ISBN 0-930934-52-0   9.95 _____
____   Cloth, ISBN 0-930934-53-9   15.95 _____
Teens Parenting—Challenge of Toddlers
____   Paper, ISBN 0-930934-58-x   9.95 _____
____   Cloth, ISBN 0-930934-59-8   15.95 _____
Teens Parenting—Discipline from Birth to Three
____   Paper, ISBN 0-930934-54-7   9.95 _____
____   Cloth, ISBN 0-930934-55-5   15.95 _____
__ **VIDEO:** "Discipline from Birth to Three"   195.00 _____

                                          TOTAL   _____

Please add postage: 10% of total—Min., $2.50   _____
California residents add 7.75% sales tax   _____
                                          TOTAL   _____

Ask about quantity discounts, Teacher, Student Guides.
Prepayment requested. School/library purchase orders accepted.
If not satisfied, return in 15 days for refund.

NAME _____

ADDRESS _____